BECOMING

Who You Want to Be

GREGG LORBERBAUM

Original Artwork by *ELO*

GREENLEAF
BOOK GROUP PRESS

Published by Greenleaf Book Group Press
Austin, Texas
www.gbgpress.com

Distributed by Greenleaf Book Group

For ordering information or special discounts for bulk purchases, please contact Greenleaf Book Group at PO Box 91869, Austin, TX 78709, 512.891.6100.

Design and composition by Greenleaf Book Group and Sheila Parr
Cover design by Greenleaf Book Group and Sheila Parr
All paintings copyright © Evan Gray Lorberbaum. All rights reserved. The works may not be reproduced or distributed, in whole or in part, without the prior written permission of the artist.
Author's photo and photo of journals on inside cover by @vpvisuals.

Publisher's Cataloging-in-Publication data is available.

Print ISBN: 978-1-62634-611-6

eBook ISBN: 978-1-62634-612-3

Part of the Tree Neutral® program, which offsets the number of trees consumed in the production and printing of this book by taking proactive steps, such as planting trees in direct proportion to the number of trees used: www.treeneutral.com

TreeNeutral®

Printed in Canada on acid-free paper

19 20 21 22 23 24 25   10 9 8 7 6 5 4 3 2 1

First Edition

This book is dedicated to the memory of my parents, Leah and Donald Lorberbaum,
and to Jill, Evan, Lindsay, and Lucie.

And to those people I've coached. You have given me the opportunity to be of service,
and I hope you have learned from the insights I've shared here.

CONTENTS

PART TWO

PART THREE

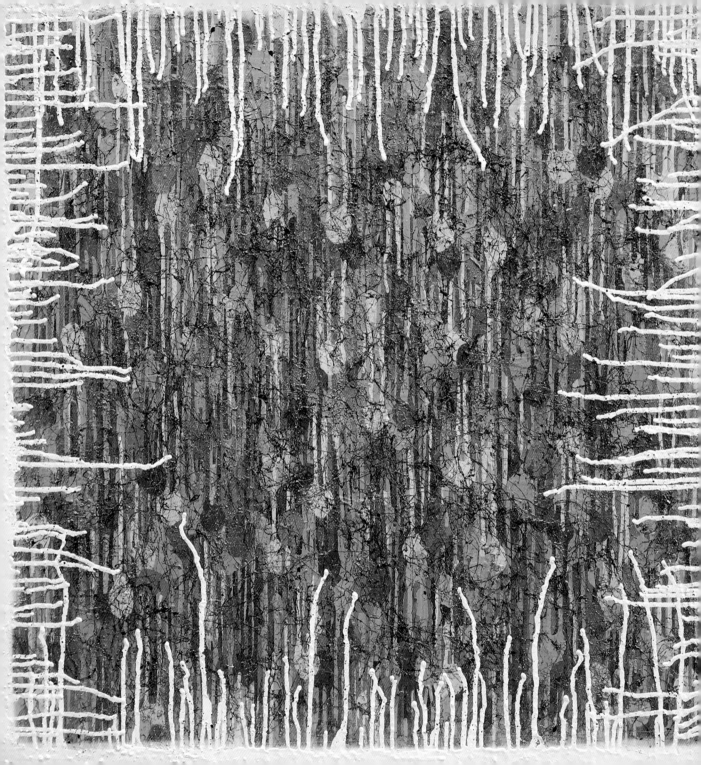

I THOUGHT I WAS SMART, BUT THE SCHOOL THOUGHT I WASN'T

"Excuse me, but you put me with the dumb kids by mistake."

Those were the words—spoken by an eight-year-old me to my teacher—that landed me in the principal's office the following day. I was sitting at the table with my alarmed mother, my second-grade teacher, Mrs. White, and my school principal, Mr. Miller. Augmenting this show of force was the school psychologist, whose name I didn't catch. This assemblage of school brass was all to address the fact that I thought I was smart, but the school thought I wasn't.

"*Please repeat what you said yesterday . . .*"

Wavery Park, my elementary school, was advanced for its time. It was 1967, and in the early sixties, "tracking" had become all the rage. Educators came up with the theory that grouping children by "ability" would benefit all the kids along the learning spectrum. As I remember it, one day my teacher divided our class into three sections—the smart kids, the moderately smart kids, and the not-so-smart kids. When she told me to go sit in the third section, my heart sank. *What if Jill, the girl I had a crush on, saw me in the third group?*

I grudgingly repeated my complaint to the group sitting at the table: I didn't belong with the dumb kids. The teacher shook her head sadly when my mother asked, "How do you know my son's not right for the group he was in?"

The discussion that followed about my reading and arithmetic problems made me even more miserable. And it led to me being subjected to a battery of tests whose results revealed that I did indeed have a cluster of learning disabilities. Most significantly, I was diagnosed with acute dyslexia, which caused me to constantly reverse numbers and letters, and to even switch the ends of sentences with the beginnings. No wonder those second-grade spelling bees were such a shame fest.

But sometimes in life, something that you think is bad turns out to be good, and what looks like an insurmountable obstacle—like a mountain with a steep, twisting path—leads to a wonderful place once you make it to the other side. That's what my dyslexia turned out to be for me. That's what your most difficult and discouraging challenges can be for you.

AUTHOR'S NOTE

I was thirty-six years old when Roger Staubach tapped me and two great partners to join him in building the New York City office of the national real estate company that bore his name. After ten years of hard work, we had grown the office from three to sixty people, and Roger, who was an icon in our industry, had built one of the most respected national real estate brokerage organizations.

In 2005, my business partners and I received a call from corporate telling us that Roger was ready to focus more of his time on charitable work: It was time for us to roll up the individually owned offices into one corporate entity—and sell. We were all on board. We knew that selling at that time was the right thing to do.

I was forty-six, and I found myself standing at a fork in the road. I knew it was time for me to leave what we had built together for years. Like a long-distance runner who decides to veer off course, I made a sharp turn away from the route. But this was no random act; I had known for a while that it was time for what I call a Role-Based Lifestyle to kick in.

My father was ill at the time, and my family needed more of me. It was time for me to alter my priorities and switch my primary role from one of office leasing broker and provider to one of son and father. Along with the reprioritization, I decided to make use of the tools I had developed along the way to create my next act. So, armed with one of those tools, the power of positive thought, I opened Centric REA, a boutique real estate brokerage firm. Having my own firm would allow me to modify my schedule to meet my new set of commitments.

I knew that it would be no easy task to compete against much larger global competitors to keep my past clients, so I assembled a great team to do just that. But I knew I needed something more, to think outside the box. I enlisted another principle—being generous in spirit—and decided to write a book. I poured a career's worth of my own proprietary processes and know-how into *Leasing NYC,* which I hoped would help young brokers coming up the ranks and NYC tenants who were looking for office space.

Leasing NYC confirmed my belief that the more you give away, the more that does come back to you, because I was rewarded in ways I had never imagined. The power of positive thought promotes the Law of Attraction, and as a result of that law, the world conspired to my advantage (just as it can for you).

I have always enjoyed mentoring people at work, and after publishing *Leasing NYC* and starting my own firm, I had the time to start what I called a "pay it forward," pro bono coaching practice. I began coaching young brokers and other people, including my son. I soon started to notice that people who used the simple process that I've laid out in *Becoming Who You Want to Be* began to be happier personally and more productive at work—regardless of their industry.

What lies within these pages is a proven system about living a role-based lifestyle, and about paying it forward to our future selves through acts of kindness and doing the things we say we will do. It's about learning from our past behaviors by keeping track of our actions. And ultimately—it's about becoming who you want to be.

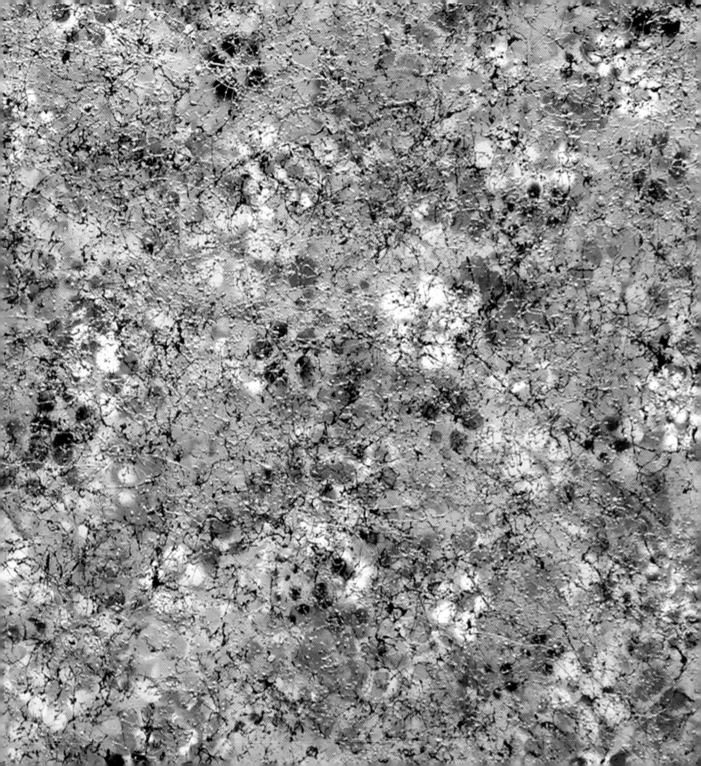

ACKNOWLEDGMENTS

Special thanks to Bob Savitt, who was my first brokerage management
consulting client, which laid the foundation for me to start my coaching practice
as a second career back in 2007.

• • •

And because life's experiences are enhanced by the presence of art and beauty,
I thank ELO for the art presented here. I hope it will be enjoyed in conjunction
with the rest of the content of this book.

• • •

Many thanks to Eti Hamlet for helping with this book and for managing
Centric Real Estate Advisors for ten years.

• • •

My thanks also go to Emily Labes and Nancy Dougherty for their contributions.

• • •

And finally, thanks to Sally Garland for her editing, Sheila Parr for this book's beautiful
design, and the rest of the Greenleaf Book Group team for making *Becoming Who You
Want to Be* come to life and for making me part of the Greenleaf family.

PART ONE

BELIEVING IN THE POWER
OF POSITIVE THOUGHT

When the doctor who tested me told my mother the diagnosis, he said that perhaps I should be prepared to live a life that would not involve "working with letters and numbers." She reacted with both dread and disbelief.

"Are you saying my son isn't mainstream?"

"Yes," the doctor said, not unkindly. "You have to tailor your expectations. If your son doesn't accept this, it could lead to other emotional issues."

"No!" she blurted out. "You're mistaken!"

"How do you know?" he asked.

"Because I know him, and I'm sure he's smart."

I know what they said, because I was present. And while it was humiliating for me, it was also the very first time I saw—and was about to feel—the power of positive thought in my life. (It wouldn't be the last.) Watching my mother stand up to the doctor was a pivotal moment for me. She simply wasn't going to permit him to tell her that I wasn't a normal kid.

The next time I saw her that resolute was during a conversation at the school, when she had to fight to keep me from being put on a lower-ability vocational track. In third through fifth grades, I heard teachers and doctors tell her time and time again that I would never be able to "succeed in an office environment."

But rather than take these conversations as devastating blows, my mother turned them around and used them as incentives to make sure I was going to prove everyone wrong.

Both of my parents had a powerful belief in me. They told me that if I worked hard, I would succeed in spite of my challenges. And I believed them. My mother was the one in the trenches day after day. She found a specialist in learning disabilities who gave us hope that if I applied myself diligently enough, I could and would increase my abilities. I went to his office regularly for audiovisual training sessions, where my challenge was to quickly identify numbers he flashed on a screen and to try to train my eyes not to reverse them (which felt difficult at the time and never really worked anyway).

At my mother's insistence, the doctor also gave me exercises to do at home. Using a typical eight-year-old's logic, I thought about the times my brothers and I had wrestling matches. Before every one, I'd drink a glass of milk because I believed it would make me instantly stronger. I didn't understand that that last-minute dose of calcium couldn't possibly affect my strength, but the power of positive thought actually did enhance my ability. These exercises would prove to be my pre-wrestling glass of milk! My mother promised me that if I did them, I would get stronger, live a happy life, and be able to do all the things the school said I couldn't. I don't know whether the sessions at the doctor's or the endless homework made any technical difference in my disabilities, but I took my mother's words to heart. I took them as a guarantee.

I simply tried harder.

And what she promised turned out to be true.

The many hours I stayed inside working after school when all the neighborhood kids were out playing gave me a keen understanding that I would always have to work harder than other people. At first, this revelation discouraged me. But I kept plugging along. Over time, I found that I had a strong social sense and an ability to think fast on my feet. I worked hard at developing those qualities further to compensate for what I liked to call my "blatant deficiencies." They would serve me well.

In high school, I considered myself a success, and I went on to Tulane University. But by then, I was fully aware that I had to work harder than other students, and I knew that I would have to sacrifice and organize my life, particularly my social life, around my studies. I was also fully aware that positive thought works only with effort—and when it's coupled with a strong sense of self.

I'm not going to offer any new scientific evidence about the power of positive thinking. I'm just going to tell you about my own experiences. I have personally benefited from maintaining positive thoughts, which I define as expecting the best of myself, giving the best of myself, and expecting the best from others. I've learned the hard way that while we can't control much of what happens around us, we can control our own behaviors. I know it's easier said than done, and sometimes it's very hard to stay positive about the outcomes that we desire.

But controlling our behavior is precisely how we shape who we become and achieve the life we aspire to live. Overcoming challenges often can't be done in one leap, but rather through a series of baby steps. As we begin to appreciate the value of any struggle we are in, we learn to reinforce our constructive behaviors, and they take on their own momentum, like a snowball growing bigger and faster as it rolls down the hill.

When you're faced with a great challenge, especially as a child, it helps tremendously to have people who have faith in you and who demonstrate positive thinking for you. When I received the dyslexia diagnosis, I felt it was happening not to me—but to my parents. I wanted to make them proud, so I didn't want them to be wrong about me. I also didn't want them to be sad. Since they both believed in me, I believed in myself. My father told me to choose what

I wanted to be and to be the best I could be at it. I hope my story will inspire all the parents out there whose children have received similar diagnoses and similar dire predictions for the future. Your children's teachers and doctors aren't always right, and "bad news" isn't always what it seems.

NOTES TO MYSELF

It's New Year's Eve, and the ball in Times Square is about to drop. Another year has flown by. Most people are asking themselves, *Where has the time gone*? But unlike most people, I know *exactly* where the time has gone. This is because I have kept a journal for more than thirty-five years—accounting for nearly every single day of my life.

The impulse to keep a record of my thoughts and actions originated many years before I began journaling. I was competitive, and when I was told what I needed to do to overcome my dyslexia, I did it—and more. Some of what I did was instinctual. The rest of it was simply accepting the harsh truth that I lacked certain skills that are generally required to be successful. And I knew that I could compensate by doing whatever it was I needed to do.

When I started working with the learning disabilities tutor at age eight and doing hours of practice at home each week, I began writing down the exercises. Soon I started writing *about* the exercises. If I was supposed to do one or two, I did more. If I saw a flashcard of a cat, I would say the word and then write it down. Then I decided I would write down every flashcard word on a small piece of paper. I did the same with numbers, and slowly the length of time I needed the image to be flashed on the screen shortened. Soon I had a stack of little papers with words on them that I kept in my pocket. I remember being aware of them, and I would take them out, cross off how many words I had mastered, and calculate how fast I had learned them. I kept track of my progress. You cannot achieve a goal unless you can measure progress! Monitoring, tracking, and effort are the keys that lead to success.

I carried these little bits of paper around in my pocket, and I truly believed I was smarter because of them. I also carried them around to remind me of all the work I had done. Just as I believed that milk would make me stronger, I believed the exercises would make me a mainstream kid. And the idea of not being mainstream at the time was easier for me to deal with because I *knew* the antidote: "All I have to do is work harder." I couldn't have known it at the time, but writing about these exercises was my introduction to journaling and a glimpse into the power of positive thought.

It was the summer of my sophomore year in college when I seriously started the practice of writing things down, and it has enhanced my life immeasurably. I picked up a little book by Hugh Prather called *Notes to Myself*. Maybe I was intrigued by the subtitle, *My Struggle to Become a Person* (since, like most twenty-year-olds, that's what I was in the process of trying to do). Inside the book, I found a collection of brief thoughts and observations that Prather had jotted down about his daily behavior, his relationships, and his evolving worldview. He was writing for himself, but his concerns were ones that are shared by most of us. His openness and vulnerability inspired me to start recording my own notes to myself. I began my first journal right then, and I haven't stopped since.

Just Minutes to Track and Look Back: The System

Each day, to this day, I spend approximately five minutes writing in my journal about the previous day. (See some examples on the inside front and back covers of the book.) The content is hardly explosive or shocking. I make a simple record of my own behavior, how I spend my days, with whom, and the events, big or small, that feel important. In addition to writing an entry each day, I look back at the entry I wrote exactly one year earlier. Often I look back five or even ten years to the same date.

At the end of the week, I go over the entries to see what my best accomplishment of the week was. And at the end of each month, I review what I call "the good, the bad, and the ugly." This kind of self-reflection produces a range of emotions and constructive insights. I find comfort reading about the times I spent with people I've lost. I feel gratitude toward friends and family. I experience humility at my own impatience with others' silly behavior. I can look back on a business deal that didn't pan out and see how I might have handled things better.

Every year on or around my birthday since the age of twenty-three (more than thirty-five years ago!), I've taken a single index card and written what I call an "emotional snapshot" of where I think I am on that day to express how I feel. It's a simple process, but the results of sticking to it for so many years have been transformational. Through daily journaling, we develop a heightened ability to understand the cause and effect of our own behavior, and to see what we need to focus on if we want to achieve our life's goals.

A Precious Life Support System

Humans regularly distort our own reality—in fact, it's only natural for us to do so. When one thought or set of thoughts we believe in doesn't correspond to reality, psychologists call our reaction to this disconnect *cognitive dissonance*. It means we cannot hold two conflicting thoughts, so we adjust to the conflict by adjusting our beliefs about one of the situations.

Scientists have demonstrated over and over again how inaccurate memory can be. Without a written record to refer to, we tend to skew our memory of events in our past, sometimes so much so that we get the cast of characters or even the outcome of a certain event wrong. When we skew our own role in past events, we miss the chance to evaluate our *actual* behavior and make improvements.

Imagine a young professional from the Midwest making her first business trip to New York. From what she has read and heard, she has concluded that all New Yorkers are rude, so she braces herself. On the way to her first meeting, a stranger gives up his seat on the subway for her. When she comes out of the subway, she realizes she's lost. Another stranger notices her confusion and asks if she needs directions. When she arrives at the building for her meeting, yet another stranger holds the elevator door for her with a smile. Cognitive dissonance ensues. Either our young professional's beliefs about New Yorkers are wrong, or the New Yorkers she encounters aren't actually nice. In other words, either the impression she formed ahead of time is incorrect, or her perceptions of her experiences in the city are incorrect. Both things cannot be true. And something has to change.

But when you record your thoughts and experiences and review them regularly, you give yourself the chance to compare and contrast your beliefs with what is actually occurring. Journaling gives you the ability to look at reality and to understand personal cause and effect across the span of your life. A journal is a precious life support system that may eventually save you from future disappointment and guide your future behavior to achieve goals. I can't overstate what a profound impact keeping a journal might have on your life.

We get it, Gregg—
Journaling is your jam!
Let's move on.

TIME AND THE BLINK THEORY

As a kid, I began to experience time a bit differently from my peers. While most of my friends were pretty much living in the moment, I felt I couldn't afford that luxury. Because of my dyslexia, I knew I was going to need to plan for the future. I had to take the long view, because the daily grind was such a challenge. I knew I had to figure out what I could be, and I knew I had to find a way to make myself stand out from the others. I believed that as long as I could control my behavior and work harder than other people, I would succeed.

It's not necessarily important how you choose to make yourself stand out. Just pick something, apply yourself to it, and you will automatically end up standing out.

For example, when I became an office leasing broker, I memorized the locations and other pertinent facts about hundreds of buildings in Manhattan as a way to stand out from other brokers.

Back to the nature of time. Everyone—especially those of us with children—is familiar with the elastic nature of time: how an hour can seem to last a century, and yet a year can fly by in the blink of an eye. The trick and the challenge are to capture that blink. Many years ago, I began making an annual visit to Atlantic Beach on Long Island (where I spent my early childhood with my family.) The place seems timeless. I gaze out at the jetties, close my eyes, and open them again. The jetties remain the same year after year; I am what changes. Each year, I use this visit to contemplate how I've grown since the previous year—through effort, reflection, and deferred gratification. Those jetties have become a kind of touchstone.

On my son Evan's twenty-second birthday, I took him to Atlantic Beach. On his twenty-third birthday, we returned. Yes, the jetties still looked the same, the air smelled the same, the moss was still the same stunning shade of blue-green, and the tides still rose and fell in the same exact manner. It was the perfect opportunity for us to reflect and nourish ourselves. On that second visit, Evan and I talked about what he'd achieved and the sacrifices he had made over the past year to reach his goals. I saw this discussion as a kind of gift to my son. I introduced him to a practice that enables us to take a snapshot in time of where we have been and where we are now. When my daughters, Lindsay and Lucie, turn twenty-two, I'll share the same gift with them. This is the kind of gift we can all give to ourselves and to the people we love.

There is great value in being and living in the present, rather than torturing ourselves over past events we can't change—or tying ourselves in knots over what might or might not happen in the future. But I think anyone can benefit from experiencing time in more than one way. Once I began recording my thoughts and observations, and I developed the habit of self-reflection, I was able to appreciate the value of looking back as well as looking forward.

We grow from looking back, assessing how well we've done in the past, and from looking forward, anticipating how our present efforts will pay off in the future. Whatever I have accomplished, I attribute to the system I have developed and to my unusual perception of time.

> I was torn: I could highlight my "accomplishments" here to gain credibility with you, my reader, but I decided to spare you my braggadocio.

THREE THINGS YOU WILL DO—AND ONE YOU WON'T

I highly recommend another element of my routine that is as simple as journaling and can have just as great an impact. Each morning, make a list of three things you will do that day—and one thing you will *not*. Your task for the day—amid the whirlwind of daily demands and distractions—is to follow through on those commitments. That is, do the things you say you're going to do.

For example, my current commitments are consistent each day and entail doing a good deed (being of service), working out, and reading.

Equally important is to commit to *avoiding* one negative or unfulfilling behavior each day. If you're someone who gets upset easily, it may be in your best interest to avoid getting stressed out about the little things. Maybe you text and drive and you need to stop. Maybe you text when you're with another person. Maybe you're envious of other people's good fortune. Maybe you're too hard on yourself.

Ultimately, your commitments will depend on your values and on what you are trying to achieve. Sometimes they will remain consistent from day to day, and other times they will vary; the goal is to meet the commitments you make each day and establish a system to track your progress.

The Gift of Insight

This process of shaping your life experiences will come back to your future self in the form of insight. If you continue the practice of committing to specific actions every day, it will lead you (as it did me) to a full life. It won't happen overnight, but that doesn't matter. By doing what you say you're going to do, you are growing into the self you want to be. By focusing on small actions, you can evolve into the person you aspire to be and the person you, your family, and your friends deserve.

Controlling our behavior, changing old patterns, and breaking long-established habits is difficult, so don't expect perfection right out of the gate. Many of us have formed bad habits over the years. Whatever our vice, we tend to allow it to go unchecked if we're succeeding in our lives overall despite this behavior. The classic song "The Gambler" comes to mind. If you're gambling in a Vegas casino and you're up, you haven't won yet. In fact, you will not win until you stop and walk out the door. The song tells us that we need to know when to fold. Sometimes, your best judgment isn't about starting something new, but rather stopping something old.

Sometimes taking on a small physical challenge can help a person begin to change. For example, I ask the young people I coach to begin by doing six push-ups, and then to add one push-up each day. What you choose to do obviously depends on your fitness level. The commitment is more important than the exercise itself. The next step is to layer other simple tasks on top of your physical challenge—such as making your bed or flossing daily—in order to activate "operant conditioning." Operant conditioning is a kind of behavior modification in which behaviors are reinforced by consequences every time they are exhibited, so that you associate pleasure with a positive behavior or displeasure with a negative behavior. You start to get addicted to feeling good, but only if the accomplishment is worthy and you are adding on tasks—especially those you do for others (in what I call a role-based lifestyle). That's when other people start responding to your goodness, and suddenly your life is better. In my career as a broker, I kept raising the bar for myself; I wanted the brokers I trained to also raise the bar for themselves and to have the feeling that not catching up was a good thing. Being exhausted can be a good thing and the reward for a great effort.

Whatever we do, we become accustomed to our habits (bad or good). Habits are easier to form than most people might think (and much harder to break). Forming good habits, even simple ones, trains us to be consistent and gives us the ability to follow through on our bigger commitments. When we're working out, the last rep is the one we get most of the benefit from.

Consider this: If you were going to chop down a tree, you wouldn't swing the axe and knock it down with one blow. You would chip away at the trunk, hitting it many times until the tree fell. Having confidence in your process and recognizing that results won't always happen immediately is crucial to being successful. So many life accomplishments result from consistent, methodical effort, rather than taking one hard whack.

Hunting . . . for Happiness

As mammals, we are programmed to forage; it's in our nature. In the past, humans had to spend most of their waking hours foraging for food. And even though many of us are lucky enough to live in a society where we no longer have a pressing need to hunt or grow our own food, the desire to forage is still in our makeup.

Throughout the day, every day, we are still hunting. Most of us are looking for a way to earn money. For many, money means more than simply a way to pay the bills; it has become a symbol for something more fundamental we long for—*happiness*. Once we've earned enough money to support ourselves and our loved ones, we are free to seek more intangible and lasting rewards, such as good energy and karma. *The most important human currency is happiness*. If we find it and use it to do right by others, this kind of currency repays us many times over.

A ROLE-BASED LIFESTYLE

Many people who are unhappy are lacking one thing in their lives—and it's not money. It's relationships with other people. The majority of us cannot be truly content unless we are involved with other people and contributing to their happiness—just as they contribute so much to our happiness. We all exist in relation to other people, and these relationships shape and define our lives. Working on our relationships with others is key to transforming our lives and becoming happier. This is what I referred to earlier as a role-based lifestyle. We play different roles with different people in our lives. At the same time, I am a husband, a father, a friend, a colleague, a mentor, and so on. In the second and third sections of the book, we'll explore the concept of the role-based lifestyle more deeply. A key ingredient to my happiness in my role-based lifestyle is a generosity of spirit—or being of service.

One of the reasons I'm writing this book is to fulfill my role as someone who is actively contributing to the lives of those around him.

COACHING AND THE BIRTH OF THIS BOOK

One of the roles that has become important to me over the years is that of coach. My reasons for coaching are twofold. When my father passed away in 2010, I was touched to see some 650 people show up to Riverside Funeral Home to pay their respects. After the service, while our family was sitting shiva, many strangers, young and old, approached me to say what a huge impact my father had had on their lives. Only then did I realize my father had truly been a pioneer in the field of career coaching—before it even had a label. He began coaching before he had made a name for himself, and for no other reason than his desire to help people. He set a wonderful example for me.

My other motivation for coaching is that I genuinely enjoy it. Throughout my career in real estate, as broker, partner, and later, owner of a brokerage company, I have always enjoyed the protégé-mentor relationship, and I coached in a formal setting at work. After I sold my equity in Staubach, I missed that rewarding connection. Several nonprofits connected young associates looking for guidance with senior retired executives who were willing to mentor, but I've always marched to the beat of my own drum. So I did it my way.

My management consulting practice started about ten years ago when I was hired by Bob Savitt to help him build Savitt Partners, a full-service real estate brokerage and management company (which today is thriving). This was about the time I started my "pay it forward" pro bono coaching practice when a neighbor asked me to help him with a job search. That coaching expanded to include a broad array of people who were dealing with transition in their personal or professional lives. Today, I also do advisory work for start-ups and partnerships.

Making a Moral Contract

When I start coaching someone pro bono, we create what I call a "moral contract," which has three conditions. First, I ask that they do the things they say they are going to do—since this is the key to self-discipline and self-improvement. For example, if during a session, a job hunter agrees to make a list of friends and family members, write down what industries he or she is interested in, and research promising companies, and they fail to take these actions by the next meeting, that's fine. But the second time they don't make good on their commitment, I end the coaching on the spot. There's no malice; I simply recognize that if they can't follow through, they're not ready for this type of coaching.

The second condition of the contract is that they, based on an honor system, give to charity at a higher rate than they currently do. If they are not giving to charity, I ask them to start.

Finally, I ask that once they feel that they have comfortably established themselves, they help or coach at least one other person at no charge, as I have coached them. (Often this comes in the form of a request by me for someone else I am coaching.)

Mentoring doesn't only help the client. I've found that coaching, especially of young people, has helped me develop a heightened sense of empathy. It is an investment of time and energy that pays me back many times over in terms of personal growth. It has also made me a much more effective and understanding parent. Because I have communicated with and coached well over a hundred young adults the same age as my kids, I have a better understanding of my own children. Most parents don't have an accurate picture of their kids' lives, and because of that, they are less able to help them grow.

THE WAY TO WHO YOU WANT TO BE

My goal in this book is to help you make your own choices—which will lead to a more fulfilling life. You can implement the simple concepts and guiding principles here to begin achieving your objectives and having a happier life.

This book is organized into six chapters:

- **KNOWING YOURSELF**
- **UNDERSTANDING YOUR CLOSE RELATIONSHIPS**
- **UNDERSTANDING YOUR RELATIONSHIPS IN THE WORLD**
- **COMMUNICATING WITH OTHERS**
- **EXAMINING YOUR LIFE**
- **JOURNALING WITHOUT THE JOURNAL**

In each chapter, I share the insights I've gained through daily journaling, reflection, self-commitments, and relating to the people in my life. In the back of the book, you'll find practical material to help you take concrete steps toward becoming the person you hope to be. You'll find an inventory of some of my life experiences, sample coaching charts, and musings from my own journals at pivotal times.

I've tried to organize this material in a logical manner, but I encourage you to read the book gradually. Take your time, absorb the suggestions, and revisit the text again and again. The advice and insights I offer are the products of my own experiences and my reflections about them. They came to me as I needed them. As you create your own practice of reflection, your insights will come to you in the same way—suddenly—at the moment you are ready to see them. They will show you the way to become who you want to be.

CHAPTER ONE

KNOWING YOURSELF

When you're on a plane waiting for takeoff, the flight attendant always says that in case of emergency, you should secure your own oxygen mask prior to assisting others. It's good advice for the rest of life as well, and that is why I start this book with self-reflection and self-knowledge. When you know yourself better, you become more able to have successful personal and business relationships and to be of real service to other people. Changing your world begins with changing yourself.

FILLING THE VESSEL: PREPARING FOR THE FUTURE

Our life's work lies in developing ourselves and realizing our full potential. I think of humans as vessels. We spend our first twenty-five years or so developing our external shell, our container. Thereafter, we devote our time and energy to filling the vessel with all our life choices and experiences—like little pieces of paper that represent our actions.

These accumulated choices and experiences make us who we are, and gradually, one decision at a time, we become who we will be. Ultimately, we are accountable for the choices we make and the consequences of those choices. We are responsible for our future selves.

This reality becomes apparent in obvious ways when we document our decisions consistently and return to study them regularly, as I do. This is why I counsel the young people I work with to start developing their future selves early. The longer we allow ourselves to become settled in our ways, the more likely we are to wake up one day filled with regret that we failed to become the person we could have been. It's not a difficult process, and the time to act is *maybe now*. (At one point in my life, I would have said *the time to act is now!* But as I've become gentler, I now say *the time to act is maybe now—you'll know when it's the right time for you*.)

*   *   *

Not long after my son graduated from the Gallatin School at NYU, he realized he would have to give up his great apartment at Fourteenth Street and University Place in Manhattan. Evan was making the transition from college student to self-sufficient adult, and though his rent was not unreasonable, it was more than he could afford on his own. He and I brainstormed all the possible ways he could keep that apartment, and when we finally realized it didn't make sense for him to stay there, we were both disappointed.

Evan reluctantly started the challenge of looking for a new apartment—only to find one that was better for him in every way. He is an artist, and the new place was located in

> At the bottom of my vessel would be those little pieces of paper I carried around as a child reminding me of my hard work.

Bushwick, Brooklyn, one of the great street art capitals of the country. The space had recently been renovated, and he'd be sharing it with five great roommates. Best of all, the rent was way cheaper. Moving ended up being the best thing that could have happened to him.

Almost exactly a year later, Evan came to me because he was considering whether to leave his job at Sotheby's and wanted some advice. I knew the job wasn't right for him, but rather than telling him so, I showed him the journal entry I'd written when he was leaving his old apartment. At that time, I was focused on helping him appreciate what he currently had rather than mourning the perfect apartment he was losing. It hadn't occurred to me then that he'd wind up with an even better place. But he had. And as this entry reminded us both, the search for a new job could turn out equally well. This put his mind at ease. When one door closes, another door opens. It's one thing to recite that old adage, but it's quite another to have a concrete example right in front of you in black and white. This is exactly the type of insight you can gain through journaling.

When we look up at the night sky, we realize that our minds cannot grasp what the sky is "inside of." Time and the universe are infinite, and we cannot truly understand them. The abstract concepts overwhelm us. On the other hand, when we consider specific times of our lives in retrospect, they are finite and understandable. And they can guide us into the future.

THE POWER OF POSITIVE THOUGHT IS REAL

The power of positive thought comes from a deeply practical place and can be implemented through your own actions. The fact is that if you *believe* in a positive outcome, it is far more likely to happen. Few people realize how much they can accomplish when they are willing to set their minds to something. Everything you accomplish, every step you take toward your personal evolution, reaffirms your ability to grow and achieve.

But how does positive thinking work? The first part of harnessing the power of positive thought is simple—as simple as doing what you say you're going to do.

The second major component of positive thought is self-belief. The key to self-improvement lies in knowing what behaviors you should exhibit and then following through on those behaviors. When you follow through on your stated actions, you create a sense that you *deserve* a positive outcome from those actions. Following through and expecting good outcomes will shape you into someone who *earns* positive outcomes. Small steps in the direction of change will begin to transform who you are.

When I was twelve, I took karate classes. In order to get my yellow belt, the belt that follows the first belt, I had to break a pine board that was one inch thick. The secret to breaking the board is to elevate it on cinderblocks and then punch it in the direction of the grain. If you do this, it's virtually guaranteed to break. But to a kid, the task was still daunting. Our instructor told us to look *through* the wood. "If you're confident you will break the wood, you will break it," he said. "But if you're confident that you will hurt your hand, you will hurt your hand."

Fortunately, I was confident that I would break the wood—and I did. It's a simple concept: If you believe you can do something, you increase the likelihood that you'll succeed.

Positive thinking can do more than help you achieve your personal goals. By practicing positive thought, you pull people toward you. People tend to gravitate toward happy and successful people. When we engage in positive thought, we exude a certain aura that affects those around us and invites them to believe in our capabilities as much as we do. This is known as the law of attraction, a concept we'll explore further later in the book.

LIGHT THE SPARK

Changing your perceptions can activate the power of positive thought, which may dramatically change the outcome of any given situation. An anecdote from my high school days is a good illustration of how perception can determine reality. When my girlfriend, Roselle, and I broke up, I found myself twisted with heartbreak and suffering as melodramatically as only a teenager can suffer. My dad thought it would be good for me to get away, so he invited me along on his business trip to Dalton, Georgia, to visit the company's textile mill. It didn't sound like a particularly great adventure, but I agreed to go—it *would* be nice to get away.

When we arrived in Dalton, my father introduced me to a colleague. Tom, who was much younger than I expected one of my father's colleagues to be, had a magnetic personality and was someone who could talk you into anything. He invited me to dinner with his girlfriend and his girlfriend's younger sister, Julie; I reluctantly said yes.

From the moment I saw Julie, I was struck by how beautiful she was. What's more, she was a few years older than I was. Needless to say, she intimidated me. I spent the first part of dinner so nervous that I knew it was obvious to everyone at the table—which only made me *more* nervous. But when I ran into Tom in the bathroom, he slapped me on the back and told me I was doing quite well. He said, "Julie thinks you're adorable." I walked back to the table with a new sense of confidence. I was on a date, it was going well, and Roselle was in the rearview mirror.

After dinner, Julie and I went for a walk while Tom and his girlfriend went somewhere else. What followed was a passionate make-out session. When I saw Tom the next day, my unwavering grin told him how much I'd enjoyed the rest of my evening.

What surprised me was that Tom seemed to be sporting a secretive grin of his own. After some minor coaxing, he admitted that Julie hadn't actually told him that she liked me. In fact, she had made fun of my Long Island accent!

"Then why would you say that to me?" I asked.

"Your dad did that to me once," he replied with a laugh. "How do you think I met my girl-friend in the first place?"

Perceiving myself as having already made a good impression gave me the confidence to *make* a good impression. Once I believed that Julie liked me, I became somebody that Julie actually could like. Of course, Tom's little trick wouldn't have worked if there hadn't been a potential spark between Julie and me. But if he hadn't helped me overcome my anxiety, I never could have lit that spark.

RISK, ADVERSITY, AND GROWTH

You can't take it for granted that a beautiful destiny is waiting for you, no matter how positively you think. You were born with gifts, as we all are, but you must understand that the gifts you've received only have value if you put in the work to deserve them. When you put in this work, you will grow and realize your potential, and eventually, reap the rewards you've earned by using your gifts.

On the path to personal growth and success, everyone is bound to face risks and encounter adversity. These are a natural part of growth, and in fact, they *create* the conditions for growth. Struggle and strife are part of the duality of life. Sometimes a blessing can be a curse and a curse can be a blessing. A risk or challenge that frightens you can lead to an opportunity for growth. Plus, everyone faces their own unique set of challenges, whether large or small, and many of us will endure similar challenges. As you know, dyslexia played a part in many of the obstacles I encountered growing up. One of the more memorable occasions was my bar mitzvah.

The ritual requires months of preparation and is meant to be challenging. But reading aloud is inherently difficult for dyslexics, and Hebrew reads from right to left rather than left to right, which certainly doesn't make it any easier. So for me, the Torah portion of the ceremony had all the makings of a nightmare. My parents even asked me if I wanted to opt out. But I said, "I've got this." The truth was I was freaking out, trying to face my fears.

That day, as I stood on the *bimah* reading aloud to a synagogue full of family and friends, I lost my place in the text. Ours was an ultra-reformed congregation, and I knew that no one else in the room understood Hebrew—with the exception of the rabbi and cantor. Rather than lose my cool, I instantly decided to recite a different portion of the Torah that I had memorized. It wasn't quite long enough, so for about fifteen more seconds I continued chanting in a completely made-up language that I thought sounded like Hebrew.

So this is what they mean when they say "Fake it till you make it!"

Afterward, my mother, the only person besides the rabbi and cantor who realized what I'd done, pulled me aside. I was waiting for an earful. Instead she hugged me and said she was very impressed. That moment proved to her (and to me) what she'd always been right about: I would improvise when needed and become a successful man.

Although the prospect of preparing for my bar mitzvah had been daunting, the experience taught me how to use one of my most developed skills—the ability to think on my feet. Thinking fast and improvising have been invaluable to me in both my professional and my personal lives. If I hadn't faced the challenge of my bar mitzvah, I may not have been presented with the opportunity to develop this kind of skill until much later.

YOU WON'T ALWAYS GET WHAT YOU WANT

When someone I coach experiences a misfortune, I say something like this: "When dealing with challenges, recognize that in living a full life, you will eventually have to find a way to overcome enormous upsets. These may include dealing with serious medical problems, the death of your parents, the death of close friends, the loss of your job, and so on. In the same way that doing training runs prepares you for a marathon, the difficulties you're dealing with now are training you to handle the greater challenges that lie ahead."

To live your full life experience, you will not always get what you want. It's the only way to prepare you for what's next.

Many young people who come to me for coaching dislike their first jobs. I ask them to remember, "Life is a marathon, not a hundred-yard dash." When a marathon begins, hundreds—more often, thousands—of runners have to run for a good few minutes before they even get to the starting line. That is where these young people are. They may not have even gotten to the starting line of their real careers yet.

MINIMIZING THE MAXIMUM DOWNSIDE

Coaches often tell clients who are struggling to decide what to do in difficult circumstances to ask themselves, "What's the worst that can happen?" This prompts the person to assess how much risk is involved in the various choices they're confronting. I call this *minimizing the maximum downside*, and the concept applies to all areas of life and to many situations, from minor daily decisions to life-changing ones. Minimizing the maximum downside serves to counterbalance positive thinking by eliminating unbridled risk. To give an obvious example, you may feel perfectly confident that your brilliant daughter will be accepted to Yale. But wouldn't you still insist she apply to two or more safety schools?

This practice works well when you're confronted with two or more options. You consider the worst possible outcomes of each. Limit the potential damage, and move on from there. Sometimes the safe choice can be the right choice. Suppose you're running late for the train or bus one morning, but you hate to miss your daily jog. You could jog faster than usual and probably still catch the train. But which risk is worse—the tiny drop-off in fitness from missing a workout or the consequences of strolling in late to work?

Sometimes the decisions are colossal ones. My mother was battling an aggressive brain tumor and endured five surgeries. When it came time for the one significant operation, she wasn't in good enough condition to make decisions, so the surgeon discussed the pros and cons with my father, my brothers, and me. If they operated and successfully removed the entire tumor, which was on her optic nerve, it could prolong her life. If they damaged the nerve, she would wake up blind, but could still live for as much as a year. The chances of success were less than fifty-fifty. Without the surgery, she could still live about a year but wouldn't lose her sight. After a lot of agonizing, our family decided that, minimizing the maximum downside, we were not going to subject our mother to that operation. We didn't want her to have to live out the remaining months of her life completely blind.

Positive thought is a powerful tool, but it's not a magic wand. That's why we also need to minimize the maximum downside and avoid unacceptable risks.

It Could Always Be Worse

We all may be faced with situations so challenging that there seems to be no avoiding the worst possible outcome. At such times, it is especially important to remember that it could always be worse. In fact, one of the most productive things you can do is to imagine *how* it could be worse. Then you can at least appreciate that you are not truly facing the terrible scenario you've imagined.

When my father was diagnosed with pancreatic cancer, and we were told he had less than two years to live, I pictured how it would feel if we'd been told he only had *one month* to live. By comparison, two years seemed like a long time. So I made the most of it, spending three hours a day with him five days a week for the remaining twenty-two months of his life. Yes, it was tragic—but it could have been worse. As I mentioned earlier in my discussion of the role-based lifestyle, to spend this time with him was in large part why I walked away from my partnership at Staubach. My priority was to make memories instead of money.

Just Do It

Sometimes the best way to achieve a meaningful goal is to break down the process into several baby steps beforehand, and then stick to them. For each step of the way, assign yourself responsibilities and due dates—until you've completed the task. This technique can apply to looking for a new job or a new home, finishing a big work project—anything. When you break down any complex undertaking into steps and/or a to-do list, it's a lot easier to accomplish. An example of this type of chart can be found in part three of the book under the Project Management Approach. Once you lay out the process, you only need to stick to the plan and have confidence that it will work. Walk the fine line between minimizing the maximum downside and "no guts, no glory." But this will only work if you do the things you say you will.

Hindsight Can Show the Way Forward

Looking back at the outcomes of past challenging situations you've faced can be cathartic, reassuring, and most of all, instructive. I remember the first big real estate deal I closed. When the landlord's attorney sent over the lease, I literally spent the entire night going over it. By morning, I'd produced a thirty-page, handwritten memo with suggested changes and explanations. It was the best piece of work I'd ever done, and I proudly messengered it over to the client. A few hours later, I got a phone call. I was expecting to be congratulated on how great my work was. Instead, I listened to the client's furious attorney saying, "You had no right to try to practice law, your comments are out of bounds, misguided, and completely irrelevant, and you should stop trying to be something you're not!"

Because I was still a bit immature at the time, it took me a while to figure out what I'd done wrong. I realized I'd been so intent on impressing the client that I had insulted his attorney, who was getting paid well to negotiate the lease. In doing a week's work in one night at no charge (brokers earn commissions and are not paid to perform a lease review, which is often done at no charge), I created a hostile environment for a colleague. That was a valuable lesson. After that experience, I continued to scrutinize leases with the same enthusiasm and expertise, but I would call the memo a "broker's supplement" and send it only to the attorney. The goal, I came to understand, was not to try to make myself look good, but to make everyone involved in the transaction look good. Ultimately, that made me look better, and usually the attorney would tell the client that their broker did a great job and added value.

We can all take a lot of comfort in knowing that our past mistakes and disappointing outcomes are giving us the ability to make better, more informed future decisions.

DON'T SUCCEED AND FAIL SIMULTANEOUSLY

If you want to make decisions that yield the most success, you have to know yourself. Success can be elusive, and it requires alertness and self-insight as much as savvy. Beware of succeeding and failing at the same time. *What exactly does this mean?* Short-term success can blind you to the bigger picture. In my past career, for example, I saw young real estate brokers who failed to go after large transactions, but who were still successful at pitching and closing small deals. But even if these brokers do close a lot of smaller deals, the modest commissions they earn may not be enough for them to live on. And eventually they will be forced out of the business. Their successes culminate in overall failure. To put it another way, they win a lot of small-scale battles, but they lose the war. No one wants that to happen—either in their work or in their personal life. For example, someone who is looking to be the most successful person they can be might spend all their time making money but lose time with their kids. We might think our job as a parent is simply to provide material support, but it is also to provide nourishment and a foundation for our children.

The way to avoid winning-yet-losing situations is through self-knowledge. If those young brokers had enough self-knowledge to understand that they should have been paying attention to their behaviors and attitudes, they would have recognized that a lack of confidence was keeping them from tackling more lucrative deals. That recognition might well have led them to step up to the challenge. Another type of self-knowledge they lacked—like so many young people starting their careers—was the much more practical one of how to manage their finances. If they'd been closely monitoring their income versus their expenses, they would have realized sooner that closing bigger deals was not just desirable, but necessary.

INSTILLING VALUES

While walking up our very steep driveway one winter morning with my son Evan, who was five at the time, I started the practice of giving him words—as "gifts" to enhance his vocabulary. I continued to give him these "gifts" over the following months. From a huge number of possible words to choose from, I chose any word that popped into my mind and shared it. After a number of these walks, I asked Evan if he wanted to share his new words with his mom, and he said, "Sure." The words that came out of his mouth surprised even me. Of the hundreds of thousands of words I could've chosen, and that he could have heard, these were the words my five-year-old remembered:

- Strength
- Discipline
- Fortitude
- Responsibility
- Determination
- Drive

Without being conscious of it, I had chosen words that were prominent in my thoughts and important to me during our walks. I was surprised in one way, but it made sense that sub-consciously, these words would express my core values and therefore, what I wanted to pass on to my son. He is grown now, and it's clear to me that he has benefited from having these values instilled in him at an early age. When he won a first-grade reading contest, I gave him a trophy with those words engraved on it.

None of us can go back and change what we did or didn't learn in our childhoods. But it is never too late to examine our core values, to articulate what is most important to us in life, and to define our goals based on those values.

And of course, one of the words—determination—was misspelled!

CHAPTER TWO

UNDERSTANDING YOUR CLOSE RELATIONSHIPS

I magine a pond. The water is completely still. You pick up a stone and throw it in. The stone splashes and creates ripples on the water's surface, radiating outward from its point of contact. Now think of yourself as the stone that has entered the water. You are at the center of the rings of ripples. Whenever you interact with the world, you create ripples that emanate from you outward.

The first ripple, the one closest to you, symbolizes your most intimate relationships—your family and close friends. The ripples farther from the center also represent relationships—with friends, colleagues, associates from work, and acquaintances from all parts of your life. In this chapter, we'll explore relationships with the people who are closest to you.

LIVING A ROLE-BASED LIFESTYLE

People often have a difficult time balancing the many things they want to accomplish in their lives. As a way of organizing your life and the relationships in it, I like the idea of living your life based on a role-based lifestyle. Your life circumstances will naturally differ from mine, so you may choose other roles and/or prioritize them differently. In the role-based lifestyle, you get to choose the kinds of relationships you want to engage in and rank their importance, so that you can work at succeeding at each role.

Another good thing about adopting a role-based lifestyle is that it allows you to approach your challenges in bite-sized pieces that are more easily digested and easier to act upon. It enables you to focus on your roles one at a time and consciously reflect on how well you're doing in each.

My roles, in order of importance, are—

- Father
- Husband
- Son
- Brother/Uncle
- Friend
- Business Partner/Employer
- Mentor/Coach/Consultant
- Altruist/Author
- Citizen

You do not get to decide if you're succeeding in your chosen roles. The people on the receiving end do. Your kids—not you—decide whether you're being a good father; your wife decides whether you're being a good husband; your employees decide whether you're being a good boss, and so on. You are usually being judged by those around you, whether or not you're aware of it.

Family members may let you know how well you're doing, but other personal and professional relationships are less transparent when it comes to honest feedback. My point here is that you can only truly focus on succeeding in each role once you consciously adopt this perspective. It can be humbling to accept that the people on the other end of the relationship are the judges of how well you have delivered on your intentions. However, this mindset will make you work harder in each of your roles and help you to grow. Later on in this book, I'll discuss the importance of not allowing the opinions of others to weigh you down or unduly influence you. But this point is absolute: *It is not up to you to judge how you affect others*.

How do you apply this principle to your daily life? It goes back to the concept of setting yourself specific tasks and then completing them. Consider your primary roles and how well you think you are doing in them. This shouldn't just be your own opinion. You will need to use feedback from your family and friends in your assessment, and their judgments may not always be verbal. Often you will know in what way you may be letting someone down, without them having to spell it out. Other times it may take you a while to pick up on the nonverbal message, especially if someone is reluctant to be forthright with you.

I'm speaking from personal experience. I used to write in my journal about my work life. During the period when I was managing a company, the entries often described conflicts in which I always believed I was right. I also expressed frustration that people seemed unable to meet my expectations. For example, I held morning meetings, and some people would show up five, ten, even fifteen minutes late. This seemed disrespectful to the rest of us who were there on time, and I didn't want to establish lateness as the company norm. So I announced that the conference room door would close at eight thirty and anyone not inside at that time would be fined a hundred dollars, which would go toward a fund for a yearly company event.

But this policy didn't solve the problem. Eventually, I recognized that *I* was a part of the problem, because I was being too rigid. It was not so much what I was asking, but how I was asking it. Employees—and especially those who work on commission—resent edicts from above. They want to be part of the decision-making process. If they participate in making the rules, they are far more likely to follow them, with fewer resentments.

In my coaching practice, I've worked with several people with "big personalities" who have start-up businesses. When they complain, as they frequently do, about the incompetent intern, the employee who can't take directions, the manager who doesn't listen, the department that falls short—I think every single time, *The problem is partially you*. So I wait for the appropriate moment, and then I gently, subtly suggest that thought to them. I know about all of this because at one time, the problem *was* me. An aha moment often occurs when you realize that you are either contributing to the problem or completely creating it. My aha moment was when I realized I was creating the problem at work.

Follow-through is essential if you want to improve your roles either personally or professionally. If you forget to pay for something in a store and walk out with it, alarms will sound and a commotion will ensue. And when you don't do the things you say you're going to do in your life roles, similar alarms sound with family, friends, and coworkers. In order to lead a good role-based life, you must do the things you say you're going to do. And remember, although you might not like it, the judgment on whether or not you are succeeding in carrying out those things will be based on your family and friends' assessment. They make the final determination of how well you're doing in your roles, not you. The more steps you take to improve your relationships, the better you become in your roles. Gradually, as the fabric of your life grows stronger because of these improvements, you will inevitably become happier, because you are better integrated with the people who are important to you. This is a simple form of behavior modification: You practice behaviors that improve your relationships, and you're rewarded by feeling better, which, in turn, strengthens your resolve to continue the rewarding behaviors.

PIERCING THE SHELL

All of us have two sides: our external projection of who we want the world to see, and our internal concept of who we believe ourselves to be. In our daily discourse with others, we usually don't get past their projections, or shells. And that's fine, in brief exchanges, casual encounters, and other public situations where small talk is inevitable. But encased within each person's outer shell is someone who may yearn to be understood. Rather than frequent superficial encounters with projected images, our lives become more meaningful when we try to pierce other people's shells to reach the genuine people inside. To me, an honest conversation with someone—based on what is truly important to either or both of us—is infinitely more rewarding than pleasant but shallow chitchat. Such an exchange, even with a stranger, brings us closer to other people and enhances our lives.

A classic example of someone's projected image versus their real self is Oz in the movie *The Wizard of Oz*. Dorothy seeks out the "great and powerful" Oz to help her get back to Kansas and to help her friends—the cowardly lion, the scarecrow, and the tin man—with their problems. Refusing to see them, Oz thwarts and manipulates them with his scary voice, until the dog Toto pulls back a curtain to reveal a meek little man speaking into a microphone. Once exposed, the real "wizard" turns out to be just a guy from Kansas. He feels abashed and reaches out to help them all.

But here's a real-life example of what I mean. Many years ago when I was working for Staubach, I was in the process of hiring a new assistant. One morning, I got on the elevator, and two young women got on after me. I couldn't help overhearing their conversation. One woman was telling her friend about the job interview she was going to. She said she didn't know anything about real estate, so she'd have to wing it. But at least the word was that the guy she'd be working for was nice; nice, but demanding—whatever that meant . . .

I didn't say anything, but it was clear to me that this woman was interviewing to be my assistant. I found her very honest and likeable, and I looked forward to hearing from HR about her. After a few days when she didn't appear, I called and learned that HR thought it best to only hire candidates with industry experience. But I asked them to schedule an appointment for her anyway.

If I hadn't observed her being entirely genuine in the elevator, she may never have gotten the job. Of course, asking her back wasn't simply a whim on my part—after she came in and we had a laugh over the elevator incident, she explained that, in fact, she had no knowledge of real estate. But she'd had no experience with finance when she started her last job at Bear Stearns, and she'd done quite well there since she was a quick learner.

In the end, I wound up hiring her, and she did a great job working with me for eight years and became a vital part of our successful team.

THE CONCEPT OF SOCIAL TORQUE

How would you feel if you happened to flick a pebble into the air and it somehow shot over a building? Or what if you threw a Frisbee and it flew the length of a football field?

In physics, torque is a measure of how a force acting on an object can alter the dynamics of that object. The same idea can be applied in life and social situations. It's all about changing a state of inertia to something way beyond what is normal. In any given situation, you may do something that might seem small, but this action can have a significant effect on others.

One day, I was having breakfast in a local café when I noticed a man who was ready to pay. When he reached for his wallet, he realized that he had misplaced it. I was ready to pay too, so I said, "I'll get your bill. Someday, you'll get the bill for someone else." He was very gracious, and we went our separate ways.

A couple of weeks later, I was in the local branch of Wells Fargo that I use for my banking. Because of the negative publicity about the behavior of Wells Fargo, I was half considering moving my account to another bank. But for the moment, I needed to complete a complex wire transfer by the end of the day, and it was near closing time at this branch. If I didn't get the transfer done on time, my partners and the business we were working on would be negatively affected. Time was running out, and things were not moving along.

I was starting to think I was going to let my partners down, when a man approached and asked if he could help. It turned out he was not only the branch manager, but he was also the man whose breakfast bill I had paid!

He got involved right away and figured out how to accomplish the transfer expeditiously. The wire was sent, my deal closed, and I decided not to move my account from Wells Fargo. I wrote a letter to the bank commending the manager, and I found out that my letter had led to him being positively recognized within the company. He told me later that when he told his family about receiving the recognition, they were very proud of him.

So anytime you have a chance to do something for someone else—however small it may seem—the possible social torque it could create should push you toward doing it. The resulting benefits might change someone's life, and the more you give, the more will come back to you in the form of good karma.

PUT YOURSELF OUT THERE!

Inhibitions can be your enemy, and they can stifle your fun. When you make an effort to shed some of your inhibitions, you'll end up having many fun experiences to color your life. You never know what might happen when you approach a stranger or speak your mind, but odds are you will learn something. Most people can't or won't talk to strangers, either because they're nervous or uninterested. But if you don't take this risk every once in a while, you may lose out on some truly memorable interactions. As a young man, I made something of a practice of talking to strangers, and my life has been the richer for it. Now that I'm older, I find I'm more reluctant to approach someone I don't know for fear of coming across as a creepy older guy. But that's on me. I think the world would be a better place if we all reached out to strangers a bit more.

FORGING RELATIONSHIPS

When I was only five years old, I first saw a lovely little girl named Jill. Yes, Jill was the girl from second grade I didn't want to think I was stupid—and a lifelong crush began.

For me, it was literally love at first sight. At age ten, I told my mother I was going to marry Jill. I never lost sight of that goal. As of today, Jill has been my wife for thirty years, and together we have three wonderful grown children.

While my love for the woman who would become my wife remained unwavering, I certainly did not. For years, I was an accomplished dater. Using the power of positive thought, I always believed that Jill and I would inevitably end up together, but I also knew that if I forced the relationship before we were ready, it wouldn't work. Somehow as a teenager, when Jill was the belle of the ball, I had the insight not to try to date her. I was successful enough academically and comfortable socially, but I wasn't yet the person I was going to become.

When I was twenty-five, we finally began dating, but eventually we had a silly argument and broke up. I liked to date, and I liked talking with strangers. I liked finding out about people. So, over the next month, I went on exactly eleven dates with eleven different women. They all took place at *the same restaurant*—Raoul's, on Prince Street in the Soho neighborhood of New York City. I chose Raoul's because it wasn't trendy; it was simply a great quintessential NY mainstay restaurant. I sat at *the same table* with *the same waiters*, so the only variable was my date. All the staff was in on it since I knew they would treat me with special attention, and I set up the dates this way because it was important to me to set a nice tone. The staff got it that I just wanted to focus on the person I was with. This gave me the opportunity to take my mind off Jill and see if there was someone else out there for me. I enjoyed myself and met some nice women—all connections through other people—but none of them seemed right.

Then one night, I went to a party in the Hamptons, and there was Jill. I just stood there watching her. She was standing next to a guy, talking and laughing. When she reached out and touched his arm, something shot through me, and at that moment, I knew without a doubt that Jill was the one for me. I wanted and I needed to marry her. And I did.

Our love has not only endured, but through it, we have been able to create a loving family. I owe the fact that I have these most important people in my life to knowing when to wait and when to act. The power of positive thought and the law of attraction also helped me achieve this most important goal. By understanding time differently and waiting, I succeeded.

THE FIVE LOVE LANGUAGES

Whole careers and entire shelves of books have been devoted to the question of what makes a long-term relationship stable and happy. I attribute my own happy marriage to open, honest communication. I know this is easier said than done. But as I explained at the beginning of this chapter, in your role as husband or wife, you don't get to decide how well you are doing; your spouse does. You have to be able to hear their feedback and absorb it without immediately going on the defensive. Most areas of conflict in a relationship have room for compromise if both parties are motivated to keep the love alive.

The single most helpful book I can recommend to those working on relationships is *The 5 Love Languages* by Gary Chapman. The author, who has counseled couples over many years, perceives that we each experience being loved in one of five primary ways, or "languages." These are—

- Words of Affirmation
- Quality Time
- Receiving Gifts
- Acts of Service
- Physical Touch

Once a couple is past the magical period of being "in love," they often discover they don't speak the same love language. The wife, for example, may crave compliments on her cooking, words of encouragement for her challenges at work, and expressions of affection; when she doesn't get them, she feels unloved. Meanwhile, her husband, who grew up in a largely silent household, wonders why she doesn't seem to appreciate all the errands he runs for her and their kids, and why she doesn't love him enough to repay him in kind. Our preferred love languages are likely to be determined by what our parents modeled for us, and we tend to use the language of love with our spouse that we ourselves want to experience. So in the example above, the wife praises and compliments her husband because that is what she needs in order to feel loved, whereas he doesn't fully appreciate the words and wonders why she can't perform those small tasks that say "I love you" to him.

The bottom line, according to Chapman, is that if we want to be successful in our roles with our loved ones, we have to be willing to listen, to learn, and to give love in the way the person you love wants to receive it. This approach has certainly worked in my life. I love words of affirmation, but Jill likes acts of service. The mistakes that couples make is that they give the other person the thing *they* want, and that doesn't work. The logic is that we don't have to express love in the ways we want to get it back. Now I make the bed and make coffee. Jill is now using more words of affirmation, and that works for me.

SHOULD I STAY OR SHOULD I GO?

I don't consider myself a relationship guru, but I have coached and mentored many younger people over the years. Even when they start out talking to me about their professional goals, they often stray onto the subject of challenges in their personal lives. Many of them struggle with what to do about an ongoing relationship. And in the case of young adults, turmoil in their personal lives is likely to spill over and affect their performance at work.

From what I've learned over the years, if you're in a relationship and you're not sure it's the real thing, then the other person probably isn't sure, either. Every situation is different, of course. But when I've advised someone to consider breaking up, they've either moved on completely or, after a while, gotten back together happily with their ex. I rarely see a scenario where one person was heartbroken over the breakup and wanted to get back together and the other person refused to take them back over time. Sometimes, breaking up might even be a good thing. Rather than feel rejection, have the confidence that you will find the right person. Have the strength to walk away. I know a big theme in romance novels and movies is the tragedy of the "one that got away"—but in reality, does it happen? Not so much. In dating, like in nature, there is natural selection that has to do with the propagation of the species. If someone doesn't want you, you may be actually being saved from marrying or staying with the wrong person.

I tell my mentees, "You can undo leaving, but you can't undo staying." Before you commit to someone for a lifetime, you want to be as sure as possible that this is The One. If that means breaking up for now, have the confidence to know that if it's meant to be, it will work out. You may both end up missing each other, recognizing that fact, and getting back together.

IT'S ABOUT THE FIT

I consider myself lucky, because I recognized early that Jill and I would fit together well. The importance of a good fit is most obvious when you're considering committing to a long-term relationship. But the concept of fit can be a little hard to pin down. Remember that scene in the movie *Jerry Maguire*, when Tom Cruise and Renée Zellweger are in an elevator and a young couple gets on? The man turns to the woman and in sign language says, "You complete me." When someone in your life makes you feel complete, you have found a good fit. The two of you don't have to be alike; in fact, you're probably better off if you're not. Your attributes should be complementary; your strengths and weaknesses should fit together like puzzle pieces.

Years ago, when I was building a stone wall at our house, I had an epiphany. I picked up a beautiful rock, pleasingly round, but no matter how I placed it, I couldn't fit it into the space I needed to fill. I poked around and found a kind of misshapen, jagged rock, and it slid into the spot in the wall as if it had been made for that spot. And I said, "Aha!" because the parallel with couples who "fit" together seemed so perfect.

If everything is going wrong in your life but you are sharing it with the right person, you can still be happy. The shape of your life may not be to your liking, but you can still feel content in the knowledge that you've chosen to spend it with someone who fits well with you. Conversely, if everything else in your life is good but you're unhappily married, you'll still likely be sad. Even if you believe you've achieved absolute perfection in the shape of your life, you are unlikely to feel complete.

FINDING FORGIVENESS

We're all human, and we all make mistakes—which is why at some point in nearly every ongoing relationship, we're likely to find ourselves in a situation where forgiveness is called for. We each have our own views about what acts are too awful to forgive. But my bottom line is this: Whenever you can forgive another person, do it.

Some time back, a client was seeking coaching on an issue she was having with her husband. He had secretly made a large investment that went bad. He had to decide whether to accept the loss or try to fix it by doubling down. He took a lot of money from their kids' college fund and then wound up losing that as well. At that point, he had to tell his wife. She was devastated about the money—but even more about the breach of trust. He expressed great remorse and promised he would pay it back. "For a while, I just walked around furious all the time," she said. "Then I realized, if I don't forgive him, I'll keep carrying negative energy around, making everything worse; not just for him, but for me and the kids." Eventually, her husband managed to pay back all he'd taken from the college fund. Today that family is in good shape. Who knows where they'd be if she hadn't been able to let go of her resentment.

Here's another example. I faced a challenging situation many years ago with a business associate in a real estate transaction. Without going into detail, we were closing a big deal, and this person did something that I considered wrong. He knew how I felt about the action he'd taken, and I struggled with what to do next. Would I have this awkward tension with him every time I saw him and maybe make an enemy, or could I forgive him? So I told him, "I'm just going to view the way this deal went down as water under the bridge and focus instead on other positive aspects of our interactions." Forgiving him felt good. And ten years later, after I'd started my own boutique brokerage company, this person reached out and did me a huge favor in return, and we are still dear friends today.

So—whenever possible—find a way to forgive people for their transgressions. Forgiveness is a process and requires self-control. But when you forgive, you have more room for love. And more often than not, you make your whole world a better place in the process.

IT'S NOT ABOUT THE STUFF

One of the great effects of leading a role-based lifestyle is that you focus your life's energy on people and experiences—rather than on "stuff." Relationships improve with age, while most stuff does not. When you become fixated on acquiring material goods, you will likely think you always need a newer, bigger, better version. The life of consumption is never-ending. Things can't keep us happy. Memories and experiences, on the other hand, keep paying dividends our entire lives.

Because of my journaling, I saw time differently than other people, and I knew I had to make the most of it. The concept of time that I live by is one where I'm constantly paying it forward. I can't understand infinity, but time is understandable. All you have to do is make the commitment: When you write something down, you live life differently; you live your future differently; and you see time differently. So because of my notion of time and my love of the complexity and craftsmanship inherent in a watch that does not function on batteries, I became a watch collector. When I closed a significant office leasing transaction, I bought myself a watch, and I sometimes gave another to one of my partners on the deal. Until fairly recently, I tended to think of my life as equally composed of relationships, experiences, accomplishments, and material things. Then I lost a particular watch, one of my prized possessions.

But much to my surprise, I felt only mildly upset at the loss of this watch. It was another helpful reminder that material possessions are no longer an important part of my life. They are merely a garnish.

Unlike cars or watches and stuff, the value of family and friends is intangible, and it increases as time goes by. My parents raised my two brothers and me to appreciate the closeness of family. My father, who would become my idol, was often traveling when I was growing up. To make up for his frequent absences, my mother suggested that he take us on a boys' trip. We wound up going with him to Hilton Head for four days every year for twenty-seven years. After my father died, we three brothers decided to continue the tradition, and we've stayed at the same place we always did—where everyone knows us and treats us special. We've done this for the past seven years, and we plan to keep doing it—not only for our father, but for ourselves and each other.

Such family moments become treasured memories. Your brothers and sisters, if you're fortunate enough to have them, are the only other people on earth who shared the experience of growing up in your family; don't let past grievances or present differences stop you from treasuring them.

As for friends, you can make new ones, but lifelong friendships were made long ago, so keep investing in them. Remember your friends' birthdays, be there for them in the good times and especially in the bad, and grow old together with them. Old friends know where you've been, and they know how you got where you are now. To me, one of the signs of true wealth later in life is the accumulation, not of money, but of friends.

CHAPTER THREE

UNDERSTANDING YOUR RELATIONSHIPS IN THE WORLD

In the last chapter, we considered the first of the concentric rings a stone makes when it is thrown into a pond. That ring represents your close relationships. The concepts and strategies I'm going to discuss here apply to the people represented by the outer rings of ripples in your pond: more distant friends, colleagues, and acquaintances. However, you'll also find them helpful to your more intimate relationships.

The role-based lifestyle I described in chapter two is equally relevant to these more distant relationships. Remember, as before, in this exercise you don't get to decide if you've been successful in your relationships; it's up to the other person, "the recipient," to judge how well you have performed in a given role. For example, in the context of this book, you, the reader, is the *recipient* in relation to my role as the author. You decide if what I am saying is worthwhile enough to keep turning the pages. My success as an author depends on your reaction to this book.

HUMANS ARE AND ACT LIKE ANIMALS

Humans are mammals, and although we have intellects and the ability to reason, we share with our mammalian brethren the need to forage, the need for community, and the need for leadership. Consider the similarities of these scenes:

If you flew in a plane over the beach, you would notice human beings lying in groups of three to five, all facing the same direction in relation to the sun, fifteen to twenty feet away from the next group. If you flew over a beach full of seals, you'd see the same pattern.

On the vast African plain, where there's seemingly an infinite amount of space, you'll see a herd of thousands of wildebeests all running in the same direction—so close together they are practically touching. They crave physical touch, just as we humans do.

During mating season, bighorn rams will go through the painful ritual of butting heads in order to win the females in the herd. Smaller rams jump right into the fray against bigger, faster ones, although they must know they don't have a chance to dominate. Although we humans are more "civilized," we can witness similar confrontations when tensions run high enough between two people.

Like other animals, we are highly social, and we are constantly giving and responding to social cues. One quality we seek, consciously or not, is someone to provide leadership. As with animals, our social order is comprised of people suited for various roles. If you yearn to be a leader, you must develop the self-confidence and positivity to achieve that goal or you will never feel fulfilled. Naturally, there are many fewer leaders than those looking for someone to follow. A football team won't have success on the field unless it has talented players in every position—but they all have to follow when the quarterback calls the play.

LEADERSHIP, CONFIDENCE, AND DETERMINATION

There are many paths to success and fulfillment in life, and confidence and positivity are two qualities that will serve you well no matter which path you take, whether you seek to be a leader or not. And speaking of quarterbacks, as I mentioned in my author's note, I had the privilege of being business partners for ten years with one of football's Hall of Fame greats—Roger Staubach. I don't know whether leaders are born or made, but in our commercial real estate business, as in his football and Navy careers, Roger certainly conducted himself like a natural-born leader. He led by example, and personified personal and corporate integrity. His word was his bond. Just as he credited his team, the Dallas Cowboys, for his Super Bowl victories, in business he emphasized the performance of the team over the individual.

Roger exuded confidence. And as we discovered when we talked about the power of positive thinking, confidence is mostly about mind over matter. We've all seen on television or read about individuals who literally walk on hot coals or break concrete blocks with their fists. Their performances are extreme examples of putting mind over matter. But you can develop this characteristic and use it for more practical purposes than impressing people with amazing feats. The key to success in putting mind over matter is learning to control your behavior, one of the most important prerequisites to achieving any success. Controlling your behavior helps build your confidence; it also instills in you the power of positive thought.

I've worked in the commercial real estate industry for more than thirty years in a number of capacities—broker, partner, owner, consultant, and now coach—so I've seen many young people attempt to make it in this business. What I've concluded is that the most successful people are not necessarily the brightest or the quickest, the charmers or the leaders. They are the ones with determination. New business-generation programs designed for sales forces are based on a salesperson committing to making x number of calls per day for an extended period of time. The people who commit to doing this and follow through day after day, all do extremely well. I haven't seen one fail yet.

Self-control, determination, and confidence will work in virtually every area of your life, and this is a classic example of the tortoise and the hare. Salespeople who end up achieving may look like plodders. But those people who demonstrate consistency and hard work and who do what they have committed to do—or more—are the tortoises who will succeed in extraordinary numbers in any highly competitive industry.

THE LAW OF SOCIAL AMBIGUITY

In most social situations, people tend to take the path of least resistance. If you understand this law of social ambiguity, it will help you figure out how to handle yourself in new situations. Consider what happens when you're meeting someone new. If you take the initiative and extend your hand for a handshake, the other person will follow. If you go in for a fist bump, a high-five, or even a hug, that is most likely what you will get from the other person in return.

The same holds true in more complex encounters. If you decide how things will go in advance, you take the ambiguity out of the situation—at least as far as you're concerned—and that gives you a degree of control over the outcome. If you determine ahead of time what the outcome of your actions will be, most often others will follow along for the ride, because that will be the path of least resistance. If you need a service of some kind and you outline in advance *exactly* what you need, you're more likely to get what you want than if you leave it up to the other person to offer you a general outcome. So give a high-five and you'll get one back; put out there what you want, and you'll likely get it.

In this context, I want to mention something that a colleague shared with me: It takes positive thinking to the next level. I began recommending it to people I was coaching with some great results. In any situation—whether professional or personal—where you are meeting someone one-on-one and it's important to make a good impression, send the person across from you positive thoughts (providing the thoughts are genuine). For instance, in a job interview, convey to the interviewer *You're doing a great job. You must be really smart, which is why they chose you for this position,* and so on. The interviewer will unconsciously pick up on this message, feel more comfortable, and will like you more. One of my mentees recently used this technique during an important interview—and he got the job. Later, people in the company said he'd showed high likability during the interview. He told me he was sure the active positive thinking he'd employed helped him win the job.

Why would this work so well? I think there are two related reasons. First, in a one-on-one situation where both people feel invested in doing well, the person across from you is going to be especially receptive to any subliminal messages emanating from you. My mentee's interviewer would of course want a job candidate to think he's good at interviewing, so he'd be open to picking up on his interviewee's flattering thoughts, and he'd respond by liking him back.

Second, when you use this active positive thinking method on a date or with an interviewer, you feel you have a kind of secret power, which is a great confidence booster. Remember my story about traveling to Georgia as a teenager and going out to dinner with my beautiful date, who made fun of my Long Island accent? When my father's colleague falsely told me that she really did like me, I returned to the table feeling sure of myself. That confidence made me feel charming, so I acted charming, which turned the rest of the evening with her into a success.

In many social situations, your confidence (real or faked even) about how you want things to work out will have a powerful effect on the outcome. If you believe it, it will more likely come true.

Whenever you walk into an uncomfortable situation, imagine a way worse situation. A fun example: you're going to a party and you feel you don't look that great in your clothes. Imagine instead that you have a poison ivy rash across your face and neck *AND* you don't look good in your clothes. As you arrive at the party, touch your face and realize you don't have the rash. You'll suddenly feel a lot better.

The first thing you need to do is to recognize it's likely that others at the party are experiencing the same social anxiety, the same low self-esteem, and the need to be affirmed as you are. At one time or another, everyone feels socially uncomfortable.

So instead of worrying about yourself, think about affirming other people. Set out and face people, knowing that you are armed with a great social advantage—the ability to ask questions. When you focus on asking other people about themselves, you will feel more comfortable. And through the power of positive thought, it comes true: You are more comfortable and confident. Also, be grateful. Most of the people at the party live their lives with a decent safety net (we're going to a nice party, we know how we're getting home, we know we have a roof over our heads, we know we have car insurance and some money). Your life is full of things. Appreciate the things you have—versus what you want—and don't take them for granted.

DON'T GIVE CREDENCE TO AN INCOMPETENT JUDGE

One day I was driving down the highway with a close friend. He was telling me about a recent evening with a group of associates at a conference where he'd said something that was misunderstood. The attendees seemed to be mocking him, and he'd felt humiliated. While he talked, we happened to pass a gas station.

"See that guy pumping gas?" I asked.

"Yeah?" he said.

"He thinks you're an asshole."

He gave a laugh. "So what?"

"Exactly!" I said. "He's just some stranger you passed by. It doesn't matter what he thinks. And it doesn't matter what those guys at the conference think of you, either. They don't know you; they were only part of your life for a day or two. You didn't treat them badly. If their behavior is off-putting, that's *their* problem."

This advice may sound contrary to the role-based lifestyle, but it is actually consistent with it. This lifestyle is about consciously finding the right balance in how you conduct yourself. You want to be acutely aware of how the people you touch in your important roles are perceiving you. You need to be fully engaged with and accountable to your family, for example.

But you must also be true to yourself and your values, and not give credence to incompetent judges. You can't please everyone; worrying about the opinions of those who are simply passing through your life is a waste of emotion. They do not play an important role in your life, and you do not play an important role in theirs. As long as you treat them with the respect and kindness that you would afford any human being, you should try not to worry about what they think of you.

I told my friend that if his conscience was clear, there was no need for him to give the situation a second thought. They were already people he *used* to know.

Why should it mean so much that others notice us and approve of us anyway?

We care because we want the world to like us. From an early age, we like belonging to a group. You have a responsibility to treat strangers with empathy, but you don't have a responsibility to accept their judgment.

Wouldn't it be nice to believe that we're truly worthy of others' approval without having to seek it? It can be a struggle at times, but I think we all need to live according to our own standards and remain true to our own values when we're not doing the role-based lifestyle exercise. When we focus on living up to other people's expectations, we can often make them into mirrors that reflect our own insecurities.

When I turned forty, I purchased a 1957 Corvette as a present to myself. The car was not particularly expensive as vintage cars go, but I can't drive it without getting thumbs-up from other drivers and people on the street. While I enjoy their approval and appreciation, I don't need others to tell me that it's a feel-good car—I already know that because it makes me feel good when I drive it, whether or not anyone else is around to see me.

Are you seeking affirmation from others for aspects of your life that only need your own approval? To live a role-based lifestyle, you must value and respect the opinions of the people who are important to you. But you're never going to please everybody; it's not a reasonable goal. And I've found that when you're doing well, there will always be someone with something negative to say, because your success may make them uncomfortable. That is their problem, not yours.

THE SOCIAL EXCHANGE THEORY OF DATING

Life is a social exchange, and most of us package ourselves to be attractive to other people. We might do this by displaying our material possessions, our physical attributes, or certain personality traits that appeal to others. Everyone has offerings to make to those around them. Often, especially in a dating situation, in an effort to counterbalance our insecurities, we tend to be in a rush to put all our best qualities out on the table at once.

But when meeting someone for the first time, try not to feel as though you have to lead with your strongest suit. Be a little strategic, and lead with your subtler charms. If you're in great shape, save the tight shirt for the next date. If you own a Porsche, congratulations, but you don't necessarily want to pick up someone in it on the first date and come across as a show-off. Rather, win them over gradually with your personality, and then you'll have the chance to share more with them the next time.

When it comes to leading with your strong suit, two interesting journal entries come to mind.

The first involves an evening when I was a firsthand witness to a blind date. My wife, Jill, and I were out to dinner at the Waverly Inn in the West Village, where the atmosphere was intimate and the seating was tight. We were seated next to a friend of ours, who I happened to know was on a blind date. The date unfolded before my eyes and ears, and I couldn't believe what I was seeing and hearing.

Our friend, in his efforts to impress the woman, was busy regurgitating every single accolade or impressive accomplishment that he had ever had. He was quick to point out he had graduated from Harvard (forty years earlier). *Really?* He proceeded to tell her about all the money he made on bitcoin, where he travelled, his great golf game, and on and on. I watched, stunned and amazed, at how much time he spent talking about himself—and therefore, how little time he allowed the woman to reveal anything about herself.

Needless to say, that blind date didn't lead anywhere.

The second story, a complete contrast to the first, is about a young friend, Michael, who was a recent graduate of Harvard Business School.

I was at a dinner party when I overheard someone ask Michael where he had gone to school and what he was doing. Instead of saying he had just graduated from HBS, he mentioned the name of his undergraduate school. I was surprised that someone his age would have such a degree of poise to not want everyone to hear about his impressive Harvard credentials. By way of telling what he had been doing, he talked about the time he spent outside of the United States in 2012.

Prior to going to HBS, Michael spent five years in China, where he became fluent in conversational Mandarin and conducted business in the language for a privately held Chinese manufacturing company.

While there were no formal rules prohibiting ex-pats from socializing with the locals, the overwhelming majority of Americans didn't mix with the Chinese and usually stayed within the confines of a neighborhood known as Little America. One night, Michael and a friend ventured beyond their familiar surroundings and realized they were drawing quite a bit of attention from the locals—especially from two young, attractive Chinese women.

"That guy is kind of cute for a round-eye," said one of the girls in Mandarin. Of course, Michael understood what she had said.

Michael, his friend, and the two girls chatted in English, and before long, Michael and the girl, whose name was Ren, were dating. On all their dates, Michael and Ren spoke English, and Ren and her friend spoke Mandarin, fully believing that Michael didn't understand anything she was telling her friend.

After five or six dates, Ren informed Michael that her father would be joining them at a music recital they had all been invited to. Ren told Michael that her father was a successful

Chinese businessman who didn't speak English well (and resented the fact that foreigners who did business in China did not speak Chinese), so Michael should speak slowly.

When Michael was introduced to Ren's father, he responded with not only the proper and customary social gestures, but he launched into full Mandarin. The father was extremely impressed and asked why Michael had never told Ren he spoke Mandarin.

Michael said, "She never asked—and I didn't want to boast!"

It was impressive enough that he knew how to speak the language, and Ren had a new respect for Michael equal to that of her father. But the fact that Michael didn't try to impress her with his accomplishments made it that much more meaningful. (Her respect was, however, coupled with her embarrassment about him understanding every bit of slang she had spoken to her friend!)

THE TRAIN TO KYOTO?

In my sophomore year in college, I transferred to the University of Pittsburgh, where I attended a program called Semester at Sea. Instead of spending a semester abroad in one location, the students attending Semester at Sea got to make an experiential, comparative study of many countries around the world—all while circumnavigating the globe on an ocean liner. When I found out that my current school, Tulane, accepted credit from Semester as Sea, I was on my way. My parents encouraged me to do the program to help me gain experience on how to navigate in unusual circumstances and help improve my sense of direction.

When I first arrived at the ship that would be my home for the next three months, I discovered I'd been given one of the few single rooms on the ship. While this allowed me more privacy, it left me without someone to walk into the first community meeting with. When I

A bold parenting move on their part at the time!

arrived at the meeting, feeling a bit forlorn, it looked like everyone else had already formed relationships, and I'd been left out. But I worked even harder than I would have otherwise to put myself out there and talk to people. It didn't take me long to realize that none of the "friendships" were more than a few hours old, and that we were all feeling the same mix of self-consciousness and social awkwardness. We were all literally in the same boat—and we wound up sharing a great adventure together.

One of my adventures involved a train ride between Kyoto and Kobe, which was difficult to navigate due to the lack of English speakers and English signage pretty much everywhere. My travel partner and I were trying to get the bullet train back to Kyoto. We were running, and we knew that if we didn't make it, we would literally miss the boat. We got to the train station, saw the train, and started running for it. Just as we arrived, the doors closed, and the train pulled out. My survival skills came out in full force. Because I was so used to being lost, I yelled out at the top of my lungs, "Does anyone speak English? Where is the next train to Kyoto?"

Back to me from across the top of a sea of organized human chaos that is the Kobe train platform, somebody yelled back in English, "Stay where you are—the train will be right there!" It turned out that the first train had been going in the wrong direction! This is a great example of a time when something that seems bad turns out to be good.

MAINTAINING HARMONY IN FRIENDSHIPS

I love to spend time with a particular dear friend. We are comfortable talking about everything, but when he brings up the subject of his job, I don't find it particularly interesting. The last time he started talking about work, instead of mentally sighing and rolling my eyes, I caught myself. However I might feel about the subject, it was important to my friend, and because I care about him, it should be important to me. It dawned on me that if I truly valued his friendship, I needed to not just tolerate this talk; I needed to pay close attention to his thoughts about his job, which was, after all, a huge part of his life.

Another person can often serve as a mirror for us and our behavior. For instance, once when I closed a significant office-leasing deal, I mentioned it proudly to a friend. He responded by saying, "Well, I also closed a big deal." It took his bragging for me to realize that I'd put him on the defensive and made him uncomfortable by discussing my own accomplishments. So I try to think twice, say one less thing a day, and let other people affirm themselves. Complimenting them first is always another good idea.

Everyone has areas in which they can improve. When your friend's behavior starts to annoy you, ask yourself, "Do I ever act the same way?"

ACHIEVING HARMONY IN PROFESSIONAL RELATIONSHIPS

When I was in high school, I was employed all summer as a professional painter. One day, a neighbor approached me and asked if I would paint her fence after hours. She didn't want to have to use the painting company, which would have charged her a thousand dollars. I told her I could do it for one hundred dollars if I could spray-paint the fence. Once the paint dried, my neighbor noticed some drips and got upset. She felt she had paid a teenager a lot of money and expected a perfect job. From my point of view, she had hired a professional off the books and gotten her fence painted quickly for one-tenth the usual cost. With each of our expectations so out of kilter, disappointment was almost inevitable.

When negotiating a price in business, try to achieve a comfortable overlap between the highest price you're willing to pay and the lowest price the other person is willing to accept. Neither party should have to stretch too far, because if they do, it could lead to discomfort and dissatisfaction later on—particularly when you don't realize the discrepancy between your expectations and theirs.

The incident of the fence happened long before I started journaling, but I wrote it down, suspecting that someday the experience would come in handy. Many years later, I came across it. Remembering this teenage experience helped me to handle a pressing challenge at work; I had paid it forward to my future self.

At another time, I was working as an office-leasing broker and was hired by a client seeking a rare type of office space. Essentially, he was searching for a needle in a haystack. In addition to wanting highly flexible lease terms, the client wanted to pay 25 percent below the going market rent. While I was thrilled to be hired for such a complex and potentially lucrative project, my childhood memory of painting that fence gave me pause.

So, rather than simply accepting the assignment, I told the client that we needed to establish realistic parameters. I explained that I valued my relationship with him more than any potential financial benefit, and I did not want to fail to meet his expectations. I said that I could not comfortably promise to achieve his objectives, because if he attempted to go with a lower-cost space, he would almost certainly be working with a less reliable landlord—the kind who might cancel the deal at the last minute, after the client had already invested in architects and engineers. The client thanked me for my honesty. Then he switched to a broker who promised to deliver what I couldn't. The broker failed (as I predicted), and eight months later, the client returned to me with more realistic goals. Our professional relationship continued stronger than ever because I'd been straight with him from the beginning.

Recently, a young real estate broker I've been coaching asked me how to handle a similar situation. His client also wanted to lease a certain amount of space far below market rate. However, the client was his boss's friend, which heightened the tension of the situation. I advised him not to jeopardize his relationship with this important client by letting him down. He needed to express his professional opinion: What the client was looking for was not attainable. I suggested that he be honest and professional. By having such a conversation, he would be *minimizing the maximum downside*, which, as I discussed earlier, is a great way to mitigate risk.

If you know you can't achieve someone's objectives, it's best to tell them up front. It's a policy that will serve you well not only in business but in all your relationships.

AFFIRM OTHERS BY ASKING QUESTIONS

As I mentioned earlier, when you let people know you're interested in them, you affirm them. In job interviews, on dates, and in your daily interactions with everyone, the easiest way to keep the conversation going and make people feel better is to ask a lot of questions, and never hold back a kind word. Giving a sincere compliment is the easiest way to spread happiness, and it doesn't cost you anything. People tend to like you less for who you are than for how you make them feel about themselves when they are around you.

You can see all sorts of people at a gym. Some walk about confidently and clearly take pride in their bodies. Others glance around self-consciously while they work out, as though they hope no one is watching. At the gym I go to, I frequently noticed a teenager, about fourteen, who always seemed to be putting forth a great deal of effort. Every time I glanced his way, he was working up a huge sweat. One day, after I'd been away for a while, I saw he was pushing himself harder than ever and had lost a little weight.

I went over and said, "I hope you don't mind me saying so, but it looks like you've lost weight! Keep up the good work."

From then on, he showed up at the gym every single day, and he really did start to slim down. Months later, I ran into him with his father, who turned out to know a friend of mine. Our mutual friend pointed me out as the guy who had given him the incentive to keep going and to get healthy. Complimenting his efforts cost me nothing, but it had a significant impact on his life.

Friends, business associates, strangers—we're all better off if we can keep in mind that everyone is somebody's child, and treat them accordingly.

> Social torque prevails!

THINGS ARE NOT ALWAYS WHAT THEY SEEM

Society functions well when people obey the rules. But as I like to say, no one drives fifty-five all the time. We've got some wiggle room—a built-in variation of what is acceptable conduct, open to interpretation. For example, a teenager who babysits a couple of hours a week for a neighbor is technically an independent contractor and should pay taxes on their income, but I suspect few people would care if that teenaged babysitter failed to fill out a W-9. Certainly, it's important to be aware of what liberties may be taken, and when. But the bottom line is that we don't *always* need to color perfectly inside the lines.

What we say we believe and what we truly believe are not always the same thing. Life is filled with contradictions, rules, and exceptions to the rules. This is particularly evident when we look at morality. Consider the classic family film *Forrest Gump*. When Forrest's devoted mother, played by Sally Field, learns his IQ is too low for him to attend public school, she "entertains" the school principal in her bedroom. When he leaves, the principal remarks to Forrest, "Your mama sure does care about your education, son."

Forrest Gump is a universally acclaimed movie, and I've never heard anyone complain about Forrest's mother's behavior, whatever their family values might be. Because Sally Field's character was a great mother, we accept as necessary the fact that she compromised herself to give her son his best chance in life. We feel contempt for the slimy principal instead.

For that matter, consider the morally compromised characters in *Pretty Woman*, a still hugely popular R-rated film. In it, a streetwalker with a heart of gold (Julia Roberts) and a titan of industry with a heart of stone (Richard Gere) get together. What begins as a cold-blooded business transaction soon becomes much more. Audiences everywhere love this story of an unlikely couple redeemed by love and are unconcerned that they violated societal norms.

My point here is that things are not always as they seem, and people don't always act the way we expect them to or draw the same conclusions that we might. When it comes to judging others' behavior—or our own—we have to weigh love and compassion on the scales along with right and wrong. Often in intimidating situations, there may be someone who is more like you than you imagine, and things are not always what they seem.

And now I have two stories—one funny and one tender—about things, people, or situations that were not what they seemed.

Up until junior high, I was friends with other kids from my homogenous neighborhood. But in high school, I wanted to be around different types of people, so I started hanging out with the jocks (although I was never truly one of them).

I was a captain of JV lacrosse my junior year (which speaks of my undistinguished athletic career in high school) and was friends with Timmy O'Keefe ("Oak"), Michael Montgomery ("Monty"), Kevin Murphy ("Murph"), and several other guys. My high school buddies and I were known as "The Family," and we often travelled in a pack. One night when The Family was all together, I found myself at a Marshall Tucker concert at Nassau Coliseum in Long Island. We occupied the third row center, standing on the chairs like everyone else in front of us, and taking up the whole row. Everything seemed to be going well until somebody behind us yanked redheaded Timmy O'Keefe off his chair, yelling, "Sit down, Carrot Top!"

Oak was never one to shy away from a fight, and the call of "Carrot Top" sealed the name-caller's fate. He was met with Oak's fist in the face, and a fight ensued. During the whole conflict, I was looking around for someone to punch (since that's what you do in a fight—right?) There were twelve of us against a smaller number of them, and I liked the odds. Then right in front of me, I saw some guy get punched. He stood there looking at me bleary-eyed, and I thought, *This guy has been prepunched . . .* so I cocked my arm back, ready to finish off the job. I have no idea if I hit him or not, but he fell back and hit the ground right as I threw the punch. Murph saw what had happened out of the corner of his eye, and within a matter of seconds, I was being credited with having knocked the guy out with one punch! A "tough guy" was born, and I kind of liked my new reputation!

Then one day (after I had been strutting around like a badass for a month), the assistant principal and athletic director (who was the father of one of my friends) called some of us over in the cafeteria. A rival town (Oceanside) was cruising the front of the school antagonizing peo-

The Family, senior year. We rocked it!

ple ahead of a big football game between us. The principal and the athletic director were saying that some of us needed to go out front and make a show of force as a statement to defend our territory.

As the group moved toward the door, I heard the words—"BRING LORBEE!"

So there I went, and as I stood outside with my tough-guy friends, I was praying that Oceanside would drive by and keep on going, which they did—and my tough-guy reputation remained intact for the duration of high school. Whew!

• • •

And now the tender story.

The husband of a dear friend of my parents was in his mid-seventies when he passed away. He had been handsome, and I remembered hearing he was quite the ladies' man and was often seen in the company of younger women in places where married men wouldn't normally be seen. He was judged harshly, but my father remained his friend. I remember asking him, a few years before the man's death, why he was friends with such a sleazy guy. My father told me that things are not always what they seem. It was revealed at the funeral that his wife and her best friend were a gay couple, and he had stayed married to his wife to cover the fact that she was gay. As a seventy-six-year-old, she came out at his funeral.

WHEN GOOD COMES FROM BAD

When I was a junior in college, I was driving from my home in New York to New Orleans with my car loaded up with everything I was taking to college. I was somewhere in the Deep South in an old blue four-door Buick Skylark that had been my parents' family car. With 100,000 miles on it, nothing about it was particularly interesting or would draw attention—except that it had New York plates.

Then I saw the lights and heard the siren. The state trooper who approached my car had a giant beer belly and was chewing tobacco. He ordered me to get out of the car.

"What have I done wrong, officer?" I asked.

"I'm the one askin' the questions here," he replied, none too politely. "Get out of the vehicle and gimme your license."

He asked where I was coming from, and I told him that I was a student from New York on my way back to Tulane University. When he read my last name off my license, he looked at me and said, "We don't like people like you disrespecting our laws in your daddy's fancy car on your way to some fancy-ass private school."

I was getting nervous standing there outside of my car in some no-name place where I knew nobody. He proceeded to look all around inside the car, and then told me he was giving me a ticket for driving with an obstructed view (which was true, as I had my belongings piled high on the back seat). Then he said, "You're lucky I'm in a good mood, L-O-R-B-E-R *B-A-U-M*! Otherwise, you'd be in big trouble, Jewboy." Then he spit a wad of chewing tobacco that landed on the ground near my fancy Jewboy shoes (I was wearing Birkenstocks), handed me the ticket, and walked away.

Yes, this was a bad experience. But the good that came out of it is that I developed a strong sense of empapthy for those who have been victims of discrimination and an acute intolerance for prejudice by anyone against anyone.

CHAPTER FOUR

COMMUNICATING WITH OTHERS

Often, the difference between a successful, happy life and a disappointing, unhappy one is a single skill: the ability to communicate with others. People who are effective communicators are more fulfilled in their interactions than people who are not. In writing, moving a comma can change the entire meaning of a sentence. "I need to leave, Gary!" sends a very different message from "I need to leave Gary!" The nuances of verbal and nonverbal communication are equally precise. Entire books have been written on this topic, many of which go into far greater depth than I will in this chapter. However, the tools I do mention here are likely to lead to a dramatic improvement in your communication capabilities.

KNOW YOUR AUDIENCE

Strong communicators are usually strong conversationalists. The first step in being both is being attentive and conscientious. You can turn someone off in a million ways, and it's all too easy to exhibit a certain behavior that causes a communication stumble.

Most of us are aware of the basic mistakes, such as speaking too loudly, standing too close, and being overtly rude. But people have different definitions of faux pas, and the easiest way to learn them is by paying attention. I've discussed the importance of affirming others. This is one of the most necessary communication tools to make use of, regardless of who you're talking to. When you first meet someone, be sure to remember their name and say it back to them, so they know you are paying attention. Being a good listener is crucial. Not only will it help you get to know the person you are talking to better, but it will also establish a reciprocal conversation.

We know that people tend to enjoy being asked questions, because it shows we're interested in them. Asking questions can also help a conversation flow.

When someone asks how your weekend was, be sure to answer in a brief but descriptive manner, and then ask, "And how was yours?" If this seems obvious, listen and see how many people fail to reciprocate when you ask this simple question. You should note that when someone doesn't ask you back about your weekend, it often signals that they are more interested in themselves than in you.

Answering with more than a knee-jerk, "Fine, thanks," will show that you enjoy talking with this person, and that action will reinforce the message that you genuinely want to hear how their weekend was as well. Once they start talking, your job is to listen. While some of us are naturally good listeners, it doesn't come easily for everyone.

Again with asking questions? Yes, it is that important.

Say One Less Thing Every Day

We all have a lot of opinions and observations, and we're often eager to share them. But is that always such a good idea? Before you speak, stop and ask yourself, "What will I accomplish if I say what just popped into my head? And what will happen if I *don't* say it?"

For example, we all know how frustrating it can be to stand in line. Say you're in line to make a deposit at the ATM. The person in front of you seems to be taking forever, and it's on the tip of your tongue to say something like, "Am I being impatient, or are you having some kind of problem here?" But unless it's someone who obviously doesn't know what they're doing, what would be the point of saying that? The person is already trying as hard as they can. Your comment can't possibly improve the situation, and it may make it worse.

Or—and this is something I used to be guilty of—let's imagine a colleague at work has guaranteed they'll get you a report by a certain day but then stops by your office at the time it's due to say they haven't managed to finish it. You're about to blurt out, "But you promised me! How could you let me down like this?" But don't. Your coworker already knows they have failed; reinforcing the fact of their failure would probably make them resent you, rather than inspire them to perform better.

In these two examples, the negative effects of what you stop yourself from saying are pretty obvious. But what I'm suggesting takes "Look before you leap" and "Think before you speak" a bit further. Because you often don't know what the outcome of any given remark you make will be, simply commit to saying one less thing every day. If you apply this practice to your daily conversations, you will find that you say several fewer things, and thereby make fewer shallow comments, cause less unnecessary negative feeling among your friends and coworkers, and avoid other consequences you can't even predict. What I can predict is that committing to saying less will, in turn, make what you *do* say all the more effective and meaningful. Become a good listener. You've heard this many times, but it's worth repeating: You have two ears but only one mouth—for a reason.

It's a simple rule for improved communication: Every day, consciously choose to say one less thing.

State Your Intentions

Two of the most obvious yet often overlooked essentials of strong communication are honesty and forethought. Before you have a meaningful conversation with someone, do you already have an idea of how you want them to perceive you? You may even brainstorm what to say before an important conversation to make sure you come across in a certain way. But rather than make this person try to guess where you stand based on what they infer, why not just come out and tell them exactly how you'd like to come across?

For example, suppose one of my friends confides in me about something they've done that they are not proud of. If they ask for my opinion, I'll say something to the effect of "I am your ally and your advocate, and I recognize that nobody is perfect. I want you to know that I am going to be supportive rather than judgmental." That way, the discussion begins at a deeper level. Rather than having to spend time trying to figure out what my attitude will be, they immediately respond to what I'm saying. This allows both of us to get right to solving the matter at hand.

This approach doesn't only work with friends and loved ones; the business world has encouraged open communication for years. As a commercial office leasing broker, when a potential client came to me, instead of spewing all kinds of facts at them, I would first say something like "I want you to consider me an expert in this field. My job as your office leasing broker is to help you increase your firm's profits by reducing your costs to occupy office space." By saying this, the client understands who they're working with, and we can get down to business with confidence.

Do Talk to Strangers

There seems to be a common misconception that this kind of candor is only appropriate in conversations where the participants are at least somewhat acquainted. But this is not completely true. My fascination with the human condition led me to my quest to live life by getting beyond people's shells to their genuine selves. And it has also led me to discover that candor can be just as useful when talking with complete strangers.

Approaching people you don't know for anything more than a good conversation may be a lost art, but it has led me to some meaningful encounters. Long before *Humans of New York* and similar social media phenomena came into being, I kept a log of my conversations with strangers; in conjunction with my journaling, I would pick a particular topic and go around asking people their thoughts on it. In the "Conversations with Strangers" section at the end of this book, I'll go into more detail. But one of the most popular questions I asked was: "What do you think is the key to happiness?"

One hot summer day, when I was working on 58th and Madison in Manhattan, I took my lunch into Central Park. I was working on my "Conversations with Strangers" initiative at the time. (I have always been curious about what people think, and I love learning about people.)

I saw an elderly man seated on a park bench poring over a prayer book, seemingly oblivious to the heat. He was wearing a long black coat and Orthodox hat right out of *Fiddler on the Roof*, and with his long grey hair, spectacles, and prayer shawl over his shoulder, I could see he was clearly a man of faith. I was always trying to push the boundaries of what it meant to be a great communicator, and I challenged myself to talk with him without offending him. The man acknowledged me with a kind look on his face.

I approached him and told him about my little project.

I said, "You seem older and wiser than me. May I ask you a question?"

"*And vat is your qvestion?*" he asked, with a thick accent.

I looked directly into his piercing blue eyes, which seemed unaffected by age, and asked, "What do you think is the key to happiness?"

He nodded and replied without hesitation. "*That is a very good qvestion. The key to happiness is to be friends with people who have about as much money as, or a little less than you do, and for those friends to be married to women who are about as pretty or a little bit less pretty than your wife; you will be happier than otherwise.*"

"Really?!" I asked in disbelief. I'd been expecting a typical statement from such a religious-looking person—something about being of service to others or expressing gratitude to God. His statement was . . . off-putting to me because it conflicted with what I thought he would say.

I had thought I was talking to a religious person. And I didn't expect a religious person to be focusing on money and looks (which I believed were such superficial things), when I was hoping for something more powerful or deep. What he said certainly didn't come out of central casting. Maybe he was more pragmatic than religious.

I guessed I looked surprised or disappointed.

"*You asked,*" he said with a shrug.

Years later, I realized that while it might have sounded superficial or mundane at first, the rabbi's comment was one of the more insightful ones I'd ever heard. It is unfortunate but true: We constantly compare ourselves to others. Sure, his phrasing may have sounded banal, but

> This really blew me away at the time.

his point was profound: To be happy, we must appreciate what we have. Our happiness is dramatically affected by the people we spend time around. If we constantly feel inferior to our neighbors and coworkers, it's tougher to achieve contentment, so try to put some economic diversity in your life rather than associating only with people who have more than you.

ENVY AND SOCIAL COMMENTARY

Not long ago, I was in an upscale rooftop bar on Ludlow Street, on the Lower East Side in Manhattan with a view of the Empire State Building. At a nearby table, a furious young woman was yelling at her boyfriend, attacking him for flirting with her best friend and lying to her about it. Then someone approached them for a picture. They wrapped an arm around each other, leaned their heads together, and smiled like they were having the best time in the world, with the beautiful Empire State Building as a backdrop. As soon as the photographer left, she went back to berating him while he hung his head.

Thanks to the popularity of social media like Facebook and Instagram, we all now get to watch our friends' and acquaintances' highlight reels. These carefully curated experiences posted online don't include the *before* and *after* of the glamorous vacation, birthday celebration, or decadent meal. But it's the before and after—the outtakes—that tell the real story. Often, you may be the person who somebody else is envying. Just as they don't know the difficulties that go on behind closed doors in your life, the people you envy also have lives full of ups and downs and experience similar problems. And this kind of behavior is not confined to social media.

I was recently brought in to coach a young man who was dealing with a great deal of anxiety at work. Things had gotten to a point that his thoughts were debilitating—even suicidal.

We discussed his situation, and I advised him to speak with a therapist on the nature of those thoughts. I told him that while many people may have fleeting thoughts of suicide, it was not an area I was capable of advising him in. However, I did say I would be happy to offer advice on any difficulties he was having in his work situation.

We scheduled a meeting at a restaurant on Park Avenue South near his office, where he was going to be meeting a date later that evening. We had coffee and discussed his situation. When we finished our session, he said good-bye and went to sit at another table to wait for his date to arrive. I had scheduled another session with a different client in the same restaurant, so I waited for that person to arrive.

When my second client arrived, we immediately started discussing the issues he was facing. He was a young man about the same age as the previous client. At one point, he was telling me how lonely and isolated he felt. As he looked around the restaurant, his eyes landed on the young man I had just coached, who was now sitting with his attractive date, and he said, "I want to be like that guy. He's got it made."

I mention this because it is such a poignant example of how we often wish for what appears to be somebody else's perfect life. In reality, we are all likely dealing with a full range of emotions on any given day. The trick is, as I mentioned elsewhere, to appreciate what you have instead of what you want. Doing so leads to gratitude instead of envy.

As I was reminded when I came upon that old journal entry about the rabbi, we tend to judge ourselves in comparison to others. And social media makes this tendency worse by further distorting our perception of what others' lives are really like.

FOCUS ON WHAT YOU *HAVE*—NOT WHAT YOU *WANT*

My family and I live at the end of a long rural driveway. We have a view of our neighbors' lake. While we were renovating our home, we went through the trouble of relocating some high-voltage power lines that were obstructing our lake view. After considerable time and expense, we accomplished this, only to discover that one remaining wire—a cable line, not a power line, could not be easily moved.

As hard as we tried, we could not find the company responsible for relocating it. For months, whenever I looked toward the lake, my eyes would go straight to the wire, and I'd feel absolutely annoyed. Finally, I had a breakthrough and acknowledged to myself that the wire was taking up less than one percent of the view. It wasn't spoiling the beautiful scene; my bad attitude was. We eventually were able to move the cable underground, and now we appreciate the view that much more. In retrospect, that cable gave me a tremendous growing opportunity: I was learning to appreciate what I had right in front of me.

Don't let one small bad thing ruin your appreciation of all that you have before you. Learn to look beyond it—or in my case, around it.

SIMPLE SHARED EXPERIENCES

An easy way to engage people and get right to deeper communication is to quickly establish something that binds you together. Naturally, pulling a commonality out of thin air can be tricky, but there are certain notions and tendencies that most (if not all) human beings share. Sometimes, simply commenting on those similarities—particularly those that are discussed less frequently—are enough to get the ball rolling.

On a related topic, we may not want to admit it, but have you ever noticed that a certain feeling of satisfaction comes with having something that other people want? I was recently reminded of this while eating at a fast food restaurant near my office. It was a particularly hot day, and the line was even longer than usual, in spite of the restaurant's efficient system of having someone come take your order in advance so that your food is waiting for you when you reach the front of the line. After getting my lunch, I found a single vacant stool and began to eat as I gazed out the window. What was I looking at? A long line of people standing outside waiting for the food that I was enjoying at that very moment.

I turned to the man next to me, who was also eating his meal alone, and said, "Excuse me, but if you don't mind me asking, have you noticed that we get to sit down in this comfortably cool place to eat our food, while all those people are waiting for theirs in the heat outside?"

"Yeah," he said.

"And doesn't it feel good?"

He thought for a second. "It *does* feel kind of good," he conceded.

From there, we allowed ourselves to indulge in some people watching and speculating about what we saw. For example: "What do you think that guy does for a living?" "How do you think those two women are related—friends, colleagues, or sisters?" And so on.

Embarrassing as it is to admit, we were also playing *BattleBots* with humans—and speculating about which of two people would win in a fight.

This interlude felt like a microcosm of all that is good in the world; here we were, enjoying good food in a comfortable place, while other people were waiting for what we already had. What's more, we were sharing it with each other. Whether you're at a ball game, enjoying an afternoon at a country club, getting to see *Hamilton* or a movie you've been wanting to see, or even simply eating a good meal in a cool restaurant on a hot day, it feels good to be a part of the "chosen few." It's a feeling that allows you to create an instant bond with whomever you're sharing it with.

Having formed a connection, my impromptu dining companion and I went on to discuss politics, current events, and other topics like old friends. When I finished my sandwich, I gathered my trash, told the man that I had enjoyed speaking with him, and left. We parted just as we had started—as strangers. But we had enjoyed a shared experience, however brief. So much about life has to do with appreciating simple pleasures.

COMMUNICATING IN THE BUSINESS WORLD: LOOK AND LISTEN

Cultivating new relationships can get more complicated in a professional environment. This is best demonstrated during the job search. When you're not only nervous but also trying to convey that you are the best candidate for the position, it's easy to lose track of how you are coming across. This is where forethought comes into play.

I always stress the importance of presentation to the people I coach. Not just *looking* professional—though that is important—but also how they present their skills and qualifications. When I'm helping someone with a job search, at the end of our first meeting they agree to write down every question they think someone might ask them during an interview. I suggest that they Google "interview questions" on the web if that's what it takes, but ultimately they agree to come to our next meeting with fifteen *relevant* questions. Nobody is going to ask what your favorite color is, but everyone will likely ask you to describe an obstacle you've overcome.

After going over their questions at our second meeting, the mentee agrees to answer those questions in writing by our third meeting. It's better if these are handwritten, because the process allows them to study their answers. Once they are satisfied that their answers articulately and adequately explain who they are, their next assignment is to practice. A lot.

Role-play your interview with yourself or with the help of a family member or friend. However you practice, you do not want to be answering those questions aloud for the first time during an interview for your dream job. If you get asked to interview for a position you aren't sure you want, do the interview no matter what. Any experience in that realm is helpful, and if nothing else, you'll have gotten the chance to practice your interview skills. (As a side note, it's best to arrive at an interview or meeting at exactly the minute it was scheduled. This normally requires arriving early and waiting to enter.)

Part of the reason it's so critical to know your answers well is that you'll want to come across as authentic during your interview, and that will be a lot harder if it sounds as though you're trying to recall a script. But more importantly, you will harness the power of positive thought because you did the things you said that you would do, and you likely worked harder than other applicants, which is a great confidence builder. If you're comfortable with your answers and the key points you want to impress upon the hiring committee, you'll be able to focus more on how you're coming across and keep the conversation moving.

Even after you've landed the job, presentation never stops being important. And as in all types of communication, it's crucial to mind the basics. For example, one of the first lessons in cultural etiquette that we receive here in America is to make eye contact. Even though your parents may have encouraged you to do this since before you can remember, looking directly at people can still be a challenge.

That is why you should challenge yourself to leave every meeting knowing the eye color of all the people in the room. If you aren't making eye contact long enough to discern that, then you aren't making eye contact long enough. Looking someone in the eye while speaking to them is the simplest way to establish a connection.

But then look away so as not to creep someone out!

It is even possible to establish connections with others during a meeting where you personally may not have many opportunities to speak. Engaged listening is particularly useful in these situations. While you may not be able to voice your affirmation, the occasional nod of agreement can go a long way.

You can also form connections with those in your professional network over the phone, whether or not you've had any prior interaction. As I mentioned earlier, in the context of face-to-face conversation, once you've learned someone's name, be sure to repeat it back to them. It's also important to be courteous. The same advice goes for telephone conversations.

Of course, these tips alone are not enough to ensure that you will continue to grow as a communicator in the workplace. That's why we sometimes need the help of others. In fact, one of the best ways to enhance your interactions with people is to actively solicit constructive criticism from others.

THE JOB HUNT

Effort Is Time Sensitive: Do It Now!

One vital lesson I teach my coaching students is the importance of putting in as much effort as possible right at the start of a task. For example, when you're looking for a job, you are far more productive at the beginning of the search than you will be after a few months.

To demonstrate this, I ask my students to hold out their arms. "It's easy, right?" They always say yes. "Now, think about holding your arms out for three or four hours. Would that be difficult?" They always agree that it would be. The takeaway is to focus a tremendous amount of effort at the beginning, when you're still at your best.

Your New Job: There Is No Traffic Jam on the Extra Mile

The most effective strategy when starting a new job is to change your expectations about *what the company is expecting* to *what it would take to be exceptional*. Accordingly, if the hours for your new job are 9:00 a.m. to 5:00 p.m., make your hours 8:00 a.m. to 6:00 p.m. If you're a salesperson and your company sets your target at one meeting per week, set your target at two meetings per week. Immediately ratcheting up your expectations of yourself to more than what the company expects of you is the fastest track to success. As my former business partner Roger Staubach used to say, "There is no traffic jam on the extra mile." More is simply more.

If you're going to adopt this mindset, you'll first need to make an accurate assessment of your strengths and weaknesses. Engage your efforts in areas in which you are likely to succeed. In a time when every child gets a trophy just for showing up, it is important to remember that the real world is way less forgiving. Play up your natural strengths as much as possible, and be honest about your shortcomings. Personally, I mentioned how I'm somebody who realized early on that in order to overcome my learning disability, I would have to work extra hard. Conversely, my ability to relate to others comes naturally. As I often tell my coaching students, "You cannot teach a runway model how to walk that way."

PUBLIC SPEAKING PHOBIA: YOU'RE NOT THE ONLY ONE

Volumes have been written on public speaking, perhaps because it is one of the most prevalent phobias people have. While this book is about how to become a better version of yourself, I offer this one tidbit on public speaking, which just so happens to be one of the best pieces of advice I ever got. It comes to me from my dear friend Trudi Bresner, a prominent communications coach.

A few years ago, I was preparing to make a speech in conjunction with an award I had received for my book *Leasing NYC*. There were going to be over one hundred people in the room, and I was exceedingly nervous. So, as always, I started to institute my "law of one hundred," which required me to practice my speech a hundred times in the actual location where I would be giving it. This may sound unrealistic, but it wasn't that great a hardship. Every day, during the month before the speech, I would recite the three-minute speech three times in a row before I left work.

One of those evenings, I had plans to meet Trudi after work. I called her to let her know that I might be a little late. When I explained why, she offered this advice. Like many great ideas, it's beautifully simple: When speaking to a large group, make eye contact with one person at a time. This is easier than you may think, because everyone is looking at you. Complete a single thought while maintaining eye contact with this person. At the end of that thought, breathe, pick a new person, and speak directly to them. By doing this exercise, each person in the audience feels you are speaking to them. Connect to one person in order to connect to the whole audience. That speech turned out to be the best one I've ever given, and I have Trudi to thank.

GETTING PERSONAL

Cat and a String

Throughout this book, I advocate open and honest communication as the basis for healthy relationships. But when it comes to first getting to know someone romantically, like other members of the animal kingdom, humans generally practice certain rituals. Some tactical behavior can be effective when you're dating. Consider the way a cat plays with a piece of string that dangles and dances. The cat chases and jumps and bats at it, completely captivated. But if the string stops moving, the cat loses interest. Often potential romantic partners enjoy the challenge of the chase as well. If one member of a new couple shows too much enthusiasm too early in a relationship, their value may drop in the eyes of the other. Conversely, playing a little hard to get may increase their worth as partner or spouse in the eyes of the other.

Does this sound cynical? Over and over in my coaching practice I've seen this issue come up. If one member of a new couple stops "playing games" too quickly, the other member's interest starts to wane, just like the cat when the string stops dangling out of reach. Accordingly, do not get comfortable with your new girlfriend or boyfriend too quickly—particularly before you've had the chance to truly know each other. Keep the challenge alive.

The "Hand Test"

Over the years, I have discovered an odd phenomenon. Initially, I thought it might be a fluke, but it turns out to almost always hold true. I like to think of the hand test as a surefire way to see if someone in your life likes you as a friend or perhaps something more.

When the two of you are together, try to find an excuse to put your hand as close to theirs as possible (perhaps a sixteenth of an inch away)—without touching. It won't work if you accidentally touch them. If this person likes you, their fingers will brush up against yours. They won't be able to stop themselves. On the other hand, if they're not interested, they'll pull their hand away.

Signs of Affection

Arguing with someone for reasons that have nothing to do with your personal gain may sometimes be a sign of affection. After all, no argument can exist unless one person cares enough about the other to want to sway their opinion or risk having an unpleasant encounter. In this regard, victory comes not from winning, but rather from knowing someone you care about is thinking more clearly than before, and that you are now on the same page.

CHAPTER FIVE

EXAMINING YOUR LIFE

More than two thousand years ago, the philosopher Socrates said, "The unexamined life is not worth living." I take his words to mean that reflecting thoughtfully on our past experiences and behavior adds value and worth to our lives. Such contemplation helps us see where we stand in time—where we've been, where we are now, and where we're going. We all have a limited time on this earth, and gaining perspective on our own lives in the context of our pasts can help us succeed and feel more satisfied.

I didn't always think this way. Like many people, I used to focus on material success, trying to make as much money as I could, which often led to buying things I didn't need to impress people I didn't know. But at some point, by looking at my behavior with a reflective eye and by remaining open to the idea that there's a lot I could still learn—I began to change and gradually became more the person I wanted to be. By studying myself and my past mistakes, I realized that I could grow and become a better person.

It's all too easy for us to miss valuable things, even when they're sitting right in front of us. Let me give you an example. For years, I worked in my home office with my desk facing the wall. One day, a friend came in and looked around. After surveying the room, he looked at me and asked, "How come you're facing the wall? How come you're not looking out the window?" It was a good question. I'd never thought about it, although the possibility had been, quite literally, right there for ages. I moved the furniture that night, and the next morning as I sat down at my desk, I was treated to the beautiful sunrise I'd been missing all those years.

I view the practice of reflection in much the same way. It allows me to take notice of something important in an experience that I may not have noticed before, even though it was right there all along. Like some of the other suggestions I've made here to help you become all you wish to be, regular journaling is easier said than done. I believe wholeheartedly that the rewards are worth the effort. But if you've given it a good try and found you aren't able to make it a habit, you can still find ways to reflect on your past. Even without journaling, there is a way to derive some of its benefits through reflection. I've included a chart in the next chapter that you can use to do just that.

Isolating the way your views have changed on pertinent topics during the various phases of your life frames your natural evolution regarding these core aspects or values. Understanding how you've dealt with past challenges and how you are evolving in the present also helps you to anticipate what you may need in the future. In other words, you can pay the insights forward to your future self.

APPRECIATION AND GRATITUDE

Treating every experience as a potential learning opportunity and/or a chance to help others is a great first step on your way to becoming all you want to be. As I said in the introduction, being of service is now one of the most significant pursuits in my life. I'm also a father who loves to help his children. A while back, when I discovered that I could help my daughter, Lindsay, out of a jam by dropping off her rent check, I happily volunteered, even though it was an inconvenient distance from my office. I left the landlord's office feeling pretty good, having pulled through for my daughter.

As I reached the sidewalk after leaving the landlord's office, I saw a teenage boy escorting an older blind woman. She was using a cane but also holding his arm. At first glance, I assumed they must be related, although they didn't resemble one another. I watched them for a moment and realized that, in fact, they didn't know each other at all. He was simply a young man helping a blind woman because it was the right thing to do. As you know, part of the way I organize my day is by choosing three things I will do and one thing I will not. One of those three things is to be of service. So when I saw the boy was leaving, I stepped up to the couple. "Excuse me," I said. "May I be of assistance?"

Although the woman was going a few blocks out of my way, I offered to "give her a ride." She took my arm, clearly delighted at having both assistance and companionship for a bit longer. Her name was Betty, and she was on her way to the local community center. She told me she'd only become blind a few years earlier, after a disorder slowly but surely destroyed her sight. I was so taken by our conversation that I walked with her until we got off the elevator inside the community center.

That day, not only was I able to be of service twice (once to my daughter and once to Betty) and meet a fascinating individual, I was also reminded of how fortunate I am to be able to see. Nothing is guaranteed, and all we hold precious is never secure or a given. Many years before, as it happened, I wrote a brief poem in my journal about imagining blindness. It took on new meaning when I found it again after meeting Betty:

"UPON MY BLINDNESS"

Blindness and disaster have become now filled with the agony of
the unappreciated sights of yesterday.
See from me; appreciate for yourself and realize
that all that's precious is not secure.

Working Together

If you face a challenge or have some type of weakness, whether big or small (as most of us do), let other people help you. Build communities of support. When I was in college, I worked on campus so I could afford to pay for a professional typist. She typed my papers beautifully—which I could not do because of my dyslexia. But more than a business transaction for both of us and despite the forty-five-year age difference, our association became an important friendship. When you turn to others for help to compensate for your weaknesses, you come to appreciate the fact that no one works *for* anyone else; we all work together.

Karma

I believe that the greatest predictor of whether someone will achieve genuine happiness and fulfillment is whether or not they are well intentioned. The more you give to the universe, the more it comes back. Karma is almost like a currency, and the more good karma you put out there, the more you'll eventually receive. If you help others only with the intent of getting helped in return, your "good deeds" will often go unrewarded. Only when you offer help unconditionally, for the sake of helping, will the universe pay you back—in more ways than you could ever imagine. I have found that if I go out of my way to help at least one person every day, it can make all the difference to them, even if it feels insignificant to me.

People Are Watching

When traveling, it's easy to offer to help someone to place their bag into the overhead bin. One recent Amtrak ride stands out in particular. After I helped one person with their bag, another quickly appeared, and then another, and then another. By the time I took my seat, I had given at least seven people a hand with their luggage.

Not long after, I was making a presentation to a broker selection committee for a company who would eventually become one of my largest, most important clients. After my presentation, Peggy, one of the attendees, drew me aside.

"Congratulations on your presentation," she said with a smile. "You know, people are always watching."

"Well . . . thanks," I said, unsure what she meant.

"I recognize you, Gregg," she explained, "because I was on that Amtrak car last week and saw you helping one person after another put their luggage in the overhead rack. It's a privilege to work with someone who takes the time to do something like that."

And I got the deal!

A Full Range of Emotions

Reading through an old journal, I was reminded of a particular experience. I used to go to Mount Kisco, a nearby town, to pick up day laborers to help with heavy yard work. You have to know what you're doing at the day labor center. It's best to have a vehicle you don't mind people piling into. You don't discuss price. Everyone expects the same fifteen-dollar-an-hour wage, a chicken cutlet sandwich, and an Orange Crush for lunch. Once you know this, you'll know what to do when people rush up to you to ask for work.

When I reached the area where workers congregated, lots of young Ecuadorians would come running up, and I would ask who spoke English. When one said he did, I would ask him to pick two more men to come with us to work. One time, a young man spoke up and chose three people to come with us—two young laborers and an older man, probably about seventy. He was muscular and vital, with deep-set eyes that appeared to have seen their share of pain. When I said I only needed three people, the young man replied that the older man would cost me nothing—the others would share their wages with him. At one point while I worked with the crew, I asked the young man, Miguel, why he insisted on bringing the older guy. He replied, "He's not just an old guy—he's the reason we're all here." He went on to tell me how this man had worked to bring his family to the United States, and then over the course of time, he'd been responsible for forty more people becoming American citizens.

At the end of the day, I gave the group an extra tip and a six-pack of cold Coronas. The older man opened his beer and turned the cold hose over his head, surrounded by his young family. The look on his face was one of pure ecstasy. A billionaire taking a 100-foot yacht into St. Tropez could not have looked happier.

This memory struck me for two reasons. First, we can't truly judge other people. Here was an elderly man who led what on the surface seemed like a tough, hand-to-mouth existence. But within his community, he was revered and regarded as a hero. Second, we all experience the full gamut of emotions—from despair to joy. They are all equally real and valid, although what triggers them varies widely depending on our circumstances and where we are on our life's journey. How we handle the emotions we experience is what gives meaning to the adventure.

CREATE YOUR FUTURE MEMORIES

When my father was dying of pancreatic cancer, we decided our family would have Thanksgiving dinner with him at the hospital rather than eat without him at home. The hospital staff assured me they'd arrange all the details. We brought the holiday turkey with all the trimmings; worrying that they wouldn't have everything set up, I packed up our best china, glassware, a tablecloth, candles, and everything else we would need to set a beautiful table.

When we arrived, we found that the hospital had not, in fact, arranged anything. So we brought up all the supplies from the car and managed to turn my father's last Thanksgiving into a precious memory, if a bittersweet one. It was a gift I gave to my future self. If I hadn't taken the precaution of bringing our things, the experience could have been quite different. It's important to try and be aware of the significance of certain days so you can make sure they will last in your memories. We did all we could to enable my father to enjoy his last family meal. He died two weeks later.

THE LATE-NIGHT POWER OF POSITIVE THOUGHT

Creating memories isn't the only way you can take care of your future self. Recently I was working late in my office, which is located in midtown Manhattan. I was waiting for a document, which I would need to send on under my name, and then confirm that it had been returned to the people who had sent it to me. This transaction was quite time sensitive.

While I was waiting, I went to the restroom. When I came back, I realized that I had inadvertently locked my office door. Inside were my cell phone, my keys, and my wallet. It was late enough that the building's lobby had been left unattended hours earlier. As soon as I went downstairs and outside to see if I could locate anyone to help, the outer door of the building locked as well.

There I was, locked out of my office and the building, with a time-sensitive document that needed my signature. What's more, I had no cell phone to contact the people who were waiting to hear from me. Beginning to grow concerned, I decided that all I could do was use what I've been talking about here all along: the power of positive thought. I told myself that eventually, someone would walk out of the building. I would get access. I would find someone on the cleaning crew to unlock the office.

But the first member of the cleaning crew (Hector) to emerge from the building did not speak English. After a lot of gesturing back and forth, he finally understood my request. He let me back into the lobby and once we were back inside, he explained in broken English that he would lose his job if he let someone into an office, even though he did believe that it was mine. I had hit a dead end.

As I tried to figure out what to do next, the elevator door opened, and out stepped an elderly cleaning lady, whom I had just met earlier in the week. I had hosted a function, and afterward, rather than throw out the leftover food, I'd wrapped it up and offered it to her. So now she immediately recognized me and smiled. "Hey, Hector," she said, "I know him. He's okay."

This entire ordeal took around twenty minutes, and I was back in my office in time to send the document and touch base with the original sender. So in the end, everything worked out. Life is funny sometimes—and unpredictable. But on this night, as with the woman who saw me loading people's luggage on the train ride, I had paid my positive actions forward to my future self.

Choices

Knowing what you want and recognizing when to take it will have the greatest impact on your ultimate happiness. Make your choices, being mindful of what truly matters to you. Live in the now.

For example, choosing a seat on a crowded train is a microcosm of making life's choices. If you reject a seat because it's facing the wrong direction, or because someone is eating a hot dog nearby, that choice will be gone forever; someone else will grab the seat, and your option will disappear. You have to weigh your choices carefully: The smelly hot dog will surely be gone in a moment, and a seat facing backward might be better than no seat at all.

CHAPTER SIX

JOURNALING WITHOUT THE JOURNAL: MAKING AN INVENTORY OF LIFE EXPERIENCES

As I mentioned earlier, when you begin keeping a journal, you begin creating a record of your life that you can refer back to in the years to come. But if you haven't been journaling up to now, can you keep track of your life? Can you trace the trajectory of your life and your decisions before you start a daily journaling practice?

Of course you can!

The Inventory of Life Experiences below is a chart you can use to reflect on the important events and people in your life to date. For each of the age groups in the left-hand column, work your way across the chart and make notes about where you were during each of the key life categories. As you fill in the chart, you'll see the twists and turns in your life and the major decisions you made at the time. If you do begin your journaling practice, you can use the categories in the chart to help you reflect on the important things in your life.

THE INVENTORY OF LIFE EXPERIENCES

Age	Love	Challenges/Obstacles	Death	Risks
0–5				
5–10				
11–14 (Middle School)				
15–17 (High School)				
18–21 (College)				
22–24				
25–36				
37–44				
45–50				
51–60				
61–75				
76–85				

Life Experience	Accomplishments	Family	Friendship	Mistakes	Paths Not Taken

PART TWO

REVELATIONS AND MUSINGS

In this section are the original thoughts that I wrote during my reflective journaling practice. Each morning I wrote about the day before, and then I looked at my journal entry from exactly one year earlier. This practice is the foundation for the ideas presented in the first section.

Dedicating this time each day to think about what is important to you is a fundamental building block of becoming who you want to be.

These reflections and musings are organized in the following categories.

- INSIGHTS

- GRATITUDE

- MOTIVATION

- RELATIONSHIPS

- PERCEPTIONS

- INTERACTIONS

- LOVE

INSIGHTS

UNCERTAINTY

*No matter how hard you work and how alert you
are, the path to self-knowledge and success will
always be full of uncertainty and setbacks.
You don't know what you don't know.*

• • •

LESS IS MORE

*Two people are going on a long hike in the Arizona desert. One
of them has to carry a fifty-pound water pack with a tube for
easy access, because he needs to hydrate. The other person
carries only a light canteen. We become enslaved by our
possessions and our need for them. And as the journey was
easier for the person with the canteen than the person with the
pack, just like in life, your journey will be easier if you carry a
lighter burden of possessions.*

• • •

THE TRAMPOLINE THEORY

IN LIFE, AS ON A TRAMPOLINE, THE FARTHER DOWN YOU GO, THE HIGHER UP YOU BOUNCE.

STAYING TRUE

While driving, I realized that the fastest lane quickly fills in to become the most popular lane, and then shortly thereafter, the slow lane. What a perfect metaphor for staying true to your convictions.

• • •

PARTIALLY GROUNDED

Trying to hit a moving target from a moving platform is too difficult. When you are making decisions, you should always be at least partially grounded.

• • •

SELF-EVIDENT

In contrast to the role-based lifestyle, your overall quality is self-evident and not to be realized in comparison to strangers (or at their recognition).

• • •

CAUSE AND EFFECT

When we focus on the past and its consequences, we can better anticipate cause and effect, as well as the future outcome of our actions.

. . .

BREAKING BAD HABITS

Sometimes, the greatest contributor to your success is what you don't do, rather than what you do. Not having that drink before you get in the car, not late-night overeating, not speaking those angry words, can all have a far-reaching, positive effect on your life.

. . .

SPEND YOUR MONEY WISELY

The way you spend your money is as important as the way you earn it. It takes both parts of the equation to maximize value and enjoyment.

. . .

TURMOIL

Trying too hard to experience inner tranquility
invariably ignites the turmoil.

. . .

GRACE PERIOD

If you know you're not going to care about something a year
from now, try not to care about it now.

. . .

STRUCTURE

Your puppy likes the cage, and we, as human beings, as much
as we don't like to admit it, often do our best with structure.

. . .

SAILING AWAY

Imagine that you dive off a boat and are now watching it sail away. The farther it gets, the harder it is to connect with it, until it's eventually impossible. Your relationships and career are much like that boat. When making decisions regarding a particular outcome or direction, recognize that they are often time-sensitive.

• • •

ON GOD

Tonight, I made the mistake of discussing religion at a cocktail party. After enduring this conversation, I came away feeling that 90 percent of all religions are saying the same thing. The 10 percent is really cultural differences, and that's what creates friction.

• • •

GRATITUDE

GRATITUDE

*Normalcy is bliss in retrospect, and all that's
precious is not secure. So appreciate what you have,
rather than what you might want.*

• • •

GARDENING TIPS

*My gardener recently told me, "You're overwatering
your grass, which has made it dependent on way more
than it needs—just like you."*

• • •

ANTICIPATION

*Most of life feels better in anticipation and retrospect than when
it's actually happening. The secret is to appreciate the moment
for the happy memory it will soon become.*

• • •

NEAR MISSES

*Appreciate the near misses in your life for the miracles they
really are. Think of the narrow miss of a traffic accident or
lightning strike, and be grateful. Think about the "what if,"
and multiply it by the number of people you care about.*

• • •

MANNERS AND GRATITUDE

*Be aware of being friends with people who are mean or
condescending to waiters or other people who provide services
for you. Those people will likely embarrass you by association
and ultimately succumb to envy at a higher rate than the
well-mannered people you know who say please and thank you.*

• • •

MOTIVATION

POTENTIAL EQUAL TO MY DESIRE

They've given me confidence, taught me to strive,
and the right to stand where I am.
But now, those beloved accomplishments amount to
nothing more than a used resume,
a burnt piece of wood, a melted ice cube.
They are nothing more than a weak man's crutch.
Now, life is real. I am a man standing naked amongst others with
potential equal to my desire, and that knowledge as my catapult.

(written upon graduation from Tulane)

• • •

BLACK ASPHALT

Black asphalt baked by the sun burns my feet
as I walk on Harvard Yard.
Exerting a force, which negates the pain, I move onward.
As I will in the future, and as I have in the past, which has
earned me this day to walk on Harvard Yard.

• • •

FINE LINE

The accumulation of achievements that finally amount to superior accomplishments is such a gradual process, and the lines of separation so fine, that those who don't make it never understand why; and those who do smile at the sacrifices they made because they knew what it took all the time.

• • •

JUST DO IT

There's no need to make a show of your work to other people. Don't complain and don't explain; just do the things you know you should be doing. There's no reason to talk about how hard you're trying. If you really are trying, people will know, and they will see the results.

• • •

BELIEVING

Believing . . .
and thereafter achieving within those bounds,
is a must, rather than a fantasy.
Applying that confidence to my life's dreams and ambitions is
the reason for success, and my sustenance and core. And shall
always be as long as I continue
Believing . . .

• • •

INTROVERT AND GROW

Except for the memory of loved words, for this span,
I will be my universe focusing my energies within my realm,
geared toward growth and self-expansion.

• • •

TIME PASSES ON

There is no such thing as stagnation—as time passes, we are either improving or not. Either becoming better or becoming worse. With this in mind, how could it be any more obvious how someone with self-control would be spending their time?

• • •

SLOW AND STEADY

Your progress toward your goal should be shaped by your own knowledge of who you are and what your circumstances are at this moment. People develop at different speeds, and individuals grow at different rates across their lifetimes. Consider where you stand right now and how much progress you are realistically able to make.

• • •

FEELING WOBBLY

The speed at which you move forward toward your goals must vary according to your level of assurance. Pressing forward at full speed when you're feeling wobbly won't result in a good outcome. When in doubt, reduce your speed so you can devote your energies to reflection as well as progress.

• • •

STRIVE

Strive for your ambitions! Every time you don't, it confirms that you don't believe you deserve them. Furthermore, it confirms that in actuality, you aren't who you think you should be.

• • •

DON'T WAIT

We are all born with good qualities and bad. The longer you wait to develop your good qualities, the stronger your flaws will become.

• • •

DISCIPLINE REQUIRED

Learning to control your behavior is the first step on your path to having a happy life.

• • •

INDELIBLE

A day well spent lives forever. So does a day spent badly. Your insights, intentions, and ability to control your behavior will be the difference in your own life.

• • •

CHANGE NOW

The person you want to be is a fantasy now,
and that fantasy slips further away from reality
every time you say, "I'll change soon."

• • •

THE LAST REP

When you're working out, the last rep is the one
that gets you the most benefit.

• • •

FLY YOUR OWN AVATAR

As much as others can be helpful, eventually we all need to
stake our own claims, and fly our own avatar.

• • •

TO THE VICTOR GO THE SPOILS

In life, everybody doesn't get a trophy for trying out.
To the victor go the spoils.

• • •

I AM,
I AM DOING,
I SHALL,
BECOME . . .

FORETHOUGHT

If you think you will need something later, don't wait until you
need it—do it now and pay it forward to your future self.

• • •

LIVING

I am alive when I make my commitments,
but I am only LIVING when I carry through on them.

• • •

OUCH

Pain is the most underestimated catalyst for positive growth.

• • •

GOOD ENOUGH?

Is good enough—really good enough?

. . .

NO RISK, NO REWARD

If you're not willing to fall off the balance beam,
you will never be great.

. . .

ONWARD

Savor each moment for what it's worth and then move on,
using the memory as fuel and incentive to depart.

. . .

Oh, the LIFE
Places tv
You'll
Go

Eat my NICKELODEON
Shorts MAD

HELLO
DISNEY
CHANNEL

Harry Potter
LEGO

RELATIONSHIPS

IT'S ABOUT THE FIT

While building a stone wall, it's all about the fit of the next stone you're looking for, rather than the particular shape of the stone. This applies to relationships more than anything else. There is no perfect person in isolation, but rather, a great fit based upon the combination of you and someone else.

• • •

SLOW DOWN

When dating or making new friends, have the confidence to present your offerings at a more gradual pace.

• • •

ENDINGS

Time passes onward into the unknown,
preserving a niche for everything in its path.
The seasons will roll around again,
and they'll always be the same.
But for us, for now, our time is over. We must advance, knowing
that each niche is special and not quite equaled again.

• • •

CRITICISM

Everyone is a work in progress, and we can all benefit from
gentle instruction on how to improve.

• • •

FLEXIBILITY

A reed is stronger than a stick because it bends.
If you learn to be flexible with others,
they are more likely to be flexible with you.

• • •

SHARING YOUR UPS AND DOWNS

One of the cruelest things we do to each other is project a
life devoid of problems, which leads others to erroneously
believe that no one else has the same kind of issues we
do. We all have problems, and the reality is that people's
challenges are far more prevalent than we reveal to each
other. Sharing the ups and downs of your life—rather
than pretending everything is perfect all the time—can
actually bring you and your friends closer together.

• • •

PERCEPTIONS

SCENE CHANGES

*As a human being, I am stationary and specific.
The motion I know as life involves the perpetual scene changes
that create my perceptions.*

• • •

PERCEPTION

*Imagine going 60 miles per hour on a straight, standard, double-
lane highway. Easy enough? Now, imagine that same road is
fifty feet up in the air, with no guardrail. Imagine going the same
60 miles per hour, and see how you feel. Even though the road
has not become any narrower, it's completely different, and it's
your perception that has made that same task quite challenging.*

• • •

PARADOX IN MANHATTAN

On a loud, clanking subway ride to West 4th Street, I came to realize that the struggle to be perceived as a "cool person" might just be impossible to achieve because if you ever really get there, you won't know or much less care that you have.

• • •

YESTERDAY'S TOMORROW

*Yesterday's tomorrow is the wave we ride . . .
With hindsight, we know what's on the other side.*

• • •

PROPHECY

Life is a self-fulfilling prophecy.

• • •

SPLENDOR

The splendor of the moment begins when it is severed from the restricting confines of past and future and let alone to evolve.

• • •

AFTER THE FACT

Often, when you're doing well, you don't get to feel good—
feeling good comes after the fact.

• • •

START RIGHT

When you plant a sapling at a crooked angle,
it will struggle to reach the sun.

• • •

FROM WHERE I STAND

Your position determines your perspective.

• • •

CAPTURING NOW

The greatest enhancement in life will come with the ability
to capture something now and appreciate it
as the fond memory it will become.

• • •

IN THE MOMENT

When I can learn to appreciate the moment, the quality of my life will be equal to the number of experiences I've had.

• • •

FULL RANGE OF EMOTIONS

We all experience a full range of emotions from ecstasy to despair, triggered by different experiences. Regardless of the catalyst, the emotion is the same.

• • •

INTERACTIONS

AFFIRMING OTHERS

More than liking you for who you are as a person, most people tend to like you for how you make them feel about themselves when they're around you.

• • •

COLLISION

At the moment of interaction with others, stereotypical first impressions are unavoidably formed. Each participant acts on their intuition, and these actions collide to create reality.

• • •

JUST SMILE

*Nothing is more assuring than a genuine smile in your direction.
Next time you're at a party, don't pose or posture. Instead, when
you make eye contact with someone, just smile sincerely.
A smile is a magnet, and that's true across cultures.*

• • •

BARRIER IN THE PARK

*Stranger, sitting next to me. I'd love to exchange pleasantries on
this beautiful day, but unfortunately we both live in a society that
rejects the innocence of my intentions.*

• • •

FOLLOW THE LEADER

*When birds are sitting in a tree and the leader decides to fly off,
it is most comfortable for the other birds to follow. One who has
the confidence to know where he is going will naturally lead.*

• • •

STUNTED EVOLUTION

As soon as cavemen started using rocks,

they started competing about who had the bigger, better one.

Evolution has only brought us so far.

• • •

ASSUME THE BEST

If you are able to assume the best in other people,

the best is what you are more likely to get back from them.

• • •

PLEASE AND THANK YOU

The most important two words to include in your daily dialogue:

please and thank you

• • •

ONCE

We pass this way but once. The regrets we will have for not letting situations and relationships develop to their fullest potential may live to haunt us well past the aborted experience.

• • •

MORAL HIGH GROUND

The view from the moral high ground is emancipating.

• • •

COMPARTMENTALIZE

Compartmentalize your life so that problems and challenges in one area don't bleed into others.

• • •

YIELDING FEELING

It took that strangeness I felt when I said, "Yes, you're right" to make me understand how stubborn I have been as of late. Let's hope that this "yielding feeling" and I won't continue to be strangers.

• • •

MAESTRO

Communication can be compared to playing an instrument—
the sheet music may have identical notes no matter who plays it,
but it will sound different based on the musician's ability to play
the notes. When we communicate with others, how we say what
we want to say is just as important as what we want to say.

• • •

THANKS FOR THAT

Look at criticism as a gift—someone has given you the
opportunity to change and be more effective.

• • •

LIFE IS SHORT

Don't lend credence to an incompetent judge.

• • •

FINE LINE

There's a fine line between persistence and impatience, and a
fine line between confidence and arrogance. Having successful
interactions with others depends on understanding these distinctions.

• • •

ENVY

If I were a doctor, the most common strain of flu affecting my coaching practice would be envy. No matter how old we are or what our circumstances are, we all battle with occasionally feeling envious. Appreciating what you have versus what you want is easier said than done.

• • •

A MICROCOSM OF LIFE

A child playing with a skimboard at the beach constantly has to decide whether to try to maximize their ride and glide a few more inches, or whether to catch a new wave. It is the same in jobs, relationships, and many other aspects of life.

• • •

MISTAKES

Mistakes are opportunities. Never waste a mistake: Own it, understand it, and avoid making the same one again.

• • •

STAYING TRUE

*When I alter my writing so that others can understand it, I seem
to lose something in the transformation. When I alter my values,
feelings, and behaviors so others will accept them, I not only lose
something—but rather, I disappear entirely.*

• • •

PEACE ON REED BRIDGE

*On Reed Bridge I sit over the Boston River.
As the sun sets around the tower,
a blue-green sky with blinding yellow.
A crisp breeze touching lightly,
just enough for the foreigners who walked by, mixing the
languages of the world to stop and look at me and smile.
As they walked away, we knew that the sun had touched us both gently,
Confirming our human bond.
And then they disappeared.*

• • •

LOVE

CURRENCY OF LOVE

If your currency is LOVE and being of service,
then your life and everyone in your orbit gets better.

• • •

COMPASSION

Wouldn't the world be a better place if we all thought of there
being one force of love, positive energy, and karma,
where you just simply treat people how you'd like to be
treated, and you treat everybody like someone's child?

• • •

DOG LOVE IS REAL
WHAT I HAVE LEARNED FROM GEORGIA, OUR THIRTEEN-AND-A-HALF-YEAR-OLD GOLDEN RETRIEVER

DON'T OVERINDULGE THOSE YOU LOVE

Because Georgia was old, I decided to treat her to a little more dog food at each meal. She gradually gained 8.5 pounds and had a hard time walking.

• • •

EAT HEALTHY

Now as I prepare and measure out 10 ounces of her expensive, diet dog food along with ¼ cup of string beans and a dollop of turkey as garnish, I decide to eat more healthily myself. No more Diet Coke . . . for me.

• • •

MATURE RELATIONSHIPS OFFER
A DEEPER SENSE OF LOVE

Georgia doesn't wag her tale vigorously anymore when she sees me. But she stares in my eyes and gently touches her paw to my face. I know that dog love is real.

• • •

WHEN YOU HAVE LIVED A GOOD LONG LIFE, PEOPLE WILL EXPECT LESS COMPROMISE ON YOUR PART.

Georgia will lie in front of the door, and we will actually walk around the other way rather than make her get up.

• • •

WHEN PICKING YOUR SPOUSE . . .

When picking your spouse, recognize that what you are looking for in a life partner will change over the spectrum of time.

PARTNERS AT DIFFERENT AGES

When you are 20–30, you are looking for . . .   someone who is attractive, fun, and has potential.

When you are 31–40, you are looking for . . .   someone who is ambitious and stable.

When you are 41–50, you are looking for . . .   someone who is well-rounded and loyal.

When you are 51–60, you are looking for . . .   someone who is insightful.

When you are 61–70, you are looking for . . .   someone who is nurturing.

When you are 71–80, you are looking for . . .   someone who is content and happy.

When you are 81–90, you are looking for . . .   someone who is self-sufficient.

When you are 91–100, you are looking for . . .   someone who is alive.

For fun, what would your list look like?

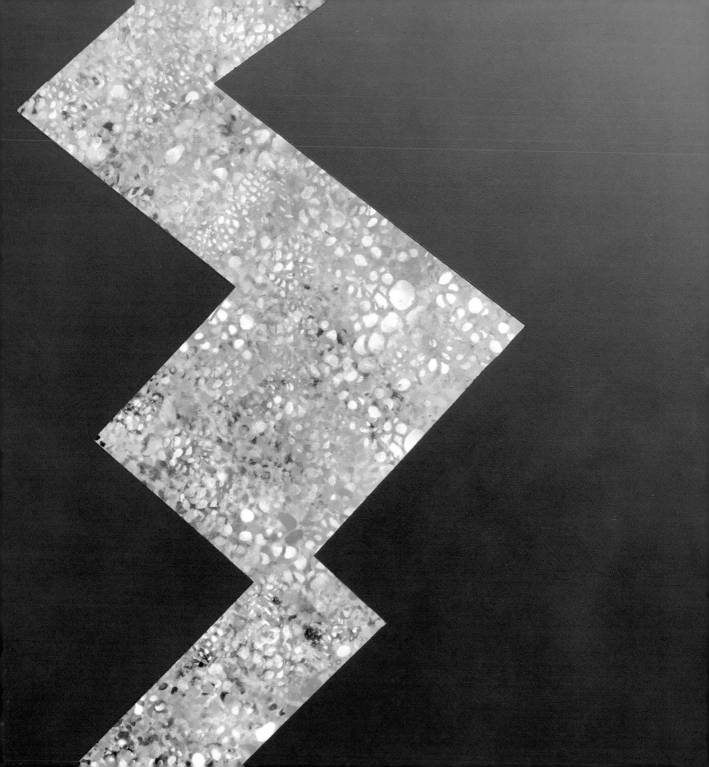

CONVERSATIONS WITH STRANGERS

The anecdotes in the preceding sections are part of my "Conversations with Strangers" project. I've spent many years—mostly in the past, when it was more socially acceptable to engage in lighthearted banter—asking strangers questions similar to the one I asked the rabbi.

Usually, I picked a specific topic on which I would question a random number of people. On the following pages is a sampling, along with the most popular answers.

CONVERSATIONS WITH STRANGERS

Could you afford your first house?

Overwhelmingly, the answer was, "No. Not even close." However, people had managed to purchase these homes anyway. My takeaway was that if I wanted to be ambitious (and avoid settling for a lesser house and then having to move not long after), I had to set my sights higher. Of everyone I asked, no one said that their lack of funds precluded them from getting a house they loved.

What is the key to happiness?

Of course, the rabbi's answer was far and away the most interesting. But it was not the only thought-provoking one I received. Many of the responses to this question were somewhat typical and were based around love and gratitude.

What is a characteristic exhibited on a date that caused you to change from thinking that the person might be "the one" to definitively knowing they were not?

Overwhelmingly, it had to do with people being bad listeners who talked mostly about themselves without asking reciprocal questions. Ostentation was also considered incredibly unattractive, as was being rude to bartenders, wait staff, and anyone else who might

Who is your best friend?

I was pleasantly surprised to find that many of the people I questioned had friends in their lives they had known since childhood.

If you are married, were you friends with your spouse before you dated?

I got a mixed response to this one, but there were many who, like me, had "played the friend card with intent." This is to say that while their romantic relationships began as friendships, they embarked on these friendships knowing that they were building foundations with the people they knew they would marry and truly wanted to get to know.

If you are divorced, did you walk down the aisle with trepidation?

The answer was almost always yes.

PART THREE

If you survey successful people (and I have), you'll find their success is seldom due to random fits and starts of effort. It's been my experience that they almost always have a larger "ordering" process in place that enables them to leverage their natural abilities. The result is a streamlined process that provides them with a competitive advantage.

Conversely, when I have spoken with or coached people facing employment challenges (such as terminations or layoffs due to their own performance), there is an overwhelming consistency in their lack of process that lends me to believe that, again, my premise is confirmed.

Decide what you will do each day, and then do the things you say you are going to do. Break up any tasks into manageable pieces, and over time, by sticking to it, you will become who you want to be.

TOOLS AND ADVICE FOR TRANSITION

Life just feels better and you are more productive when you have a solid process in place to help you achieve your objectives. Doing the things you say you are going to do will get you only so far. Effort, when coupled with process, provides the foundation for what you want to accomplish and who you want you become.

Please see the following "process docs" with their corresponding explanations to get started. These include the following:

- Three Things You Will Do/One Thing You Won't
- The Role-Based Lifestyle Exercise
- Project Management Approach
- Attributes Index Decision-Making Tool
- Pro/Con Analysis

THREE THINGS/ONE THING

Monday: Three things I will do:			One thing I won't do:

Best thing of the day:

Tuesday: Three things I will do:			One thing I won't do:

Best thing of the day:

Wednesday: Three things I will do:			One thing I won't do:

Best thing of the day:

Thursday: Three things I will do:			One thing I won't do:

Best thing of the day:

Friday: Three things I will do:			One thing I won't do:

Best thing of the day:

Best thing of the week:

Three Things You Will Do and One Thing You Won't

Times of transition are usually accompanied by uncertainty, which can be unsettling. So maintaining a positive attitude is important. One exercise that has been extremely successful is the affirmation you get by controlling your own behavior and doing the things you say you are going to do. Monitoring your behavior with a chart is helpful: By the fourth day, it will start to feel good, and this will lead to the power of positive thought.

ROLE-BASED LIFESTYLE

Please list each of the roles you are in, in order of importance.

1.	
2.	
3.	
4.	
5.	
6.	
7.	
8.	
9.	
10.	

NOTE: As a point of reference, my roles in order of importance are as follows:

1. Father
2. Husband
3. Son
4. Brother/Uncle
5. Business Partner
6. Employer
7. Friend
8. Altruist/Author
9. Citizen

Please list a specific action or actions that you could implement to be better in each of your above-stated roles.

1.	
2.	
3.	
4.	
5.	
6.	
7.	
8.	
9.	
10.	

NOTE: As an example, in my role of father, I decided to implement Thursday night comedy shows for my son Evan and me—this was in response to me wanting to make sure that we could still spend time together after he moved to the city.

NOTE: Critical to the success of this exercise is that the determination of how well you are succeeding in each of your roles is not made by you.

Role-Based Lifestyle

In transitional times, it is helpful to work on having a role-based lifestyle, which simply means dividing your life into smaller parts that are more easily digested. In this exercise, you list your roles in order of importance and then break down specific behaviors that would help you succeed in each of these roles. An important distinction to remember here is that you do not get to determine whether you have been successful in your role. You don't get to decide whether you've been a good father or son or daughter or husband: The person on the receiving end of your behavior decides that.

PROJECT MANAGEMENT APPROACH

Action Item	Due Date	Responsibility	Status/Comments

Project Management Approach

Like any other projects, transitions benefit from a "project-management approach," which compartmentalizes individual tasks with specific due dates, outlining who is responsible for each, as well as other relevant comments. This works whether you are preparing for an art show, a presentation, or making plans for a trip. It is much easier to accomplish your goals if you can see them in black and white and you can work off your list. This is doing what you say you will do. Once you put something down on paper, you can be present in other things you do, while relaxing in the knowledge of what you've done and what you need to do. When you know that you are going to do what you say you are going to do, life becomes straightforward.

Schedule, a Helpers List, Being of Service, and the Law of Attraction

During a transition, you will benefit from having a schedule that highlights the specific things you will want to accomplish and by what date.

It's not what you know; it's who you know (actually it's both). Depending on your specific circumstances, it may be helpful to make a list of "helpers." Helpers are people of influence who can help you better understand what you might want to do—i.e., they have done it before—or they are somebody who can make an introduction to someone who may be helpful.

Especially during times of transition, it is helpful to be generous in spirit and do some type of philanthropy, not-for-profit work, or anything else that you find rewarding in a feel-good way. There are emotional highs and lows associated with transition, and giving of yourself can often counteract negativity because you are helping someone else. However, an important component is that you are being of service in a genuine way and with no ulterior motive. This leads to "the power of positive thought."

A benefit of the power of positive thought is the law of attraction, in which the world conspires to your advantage. This is a direct payback for the good work that you do.

Index Decision-Making Tool and Pro/Con List

To make any decision, we are often forced to rely on our emotions. Although I am a big believer in "going with your gut," your gut makes better decisions when it can see the issues being considered in black and white. You can use these two charts together to facilitate your decision-making. You simply write down all the attributes or components of your decision. This particular attribute chart relates to a job search, but it can be modified to work on any decision you have to make. Once you have the attributes down, you can move on to the pro/con list. With the attributes, you have a weighting system that ranks the attributes by order of importance. Once you look at the two charts together, your gut can evaluate what you see as important, and it will give you a score. Use the pro/con chart to tweak your decision.

JOB SEARCH ATTRIBUTE INDEX

Score: 5-1 (5 most important / 1 least important)

	Multiplication Factor	Company 1	Company 2	Company 3
Position				
Company Reputation				
Salary				
Opportunity for Advancement				
Commute				
Physical Office Space				
Social Aspects of Work/Culture				
Flextime				
Benefits: e.g. 401(k), Health Insurance				
Totals				

Key: 1-10 (10 is the highest / 1 is the lowest.)

PRO/CON ANALYSIS

Option 1		Option 2		Option 3	
Pro	Con	Pro	Con	Pro	Con

At age twenty, I saw a young boy and an old man collecting shells down on the beach. As I ran by them, I realized that my life was going to happen in a blink—from one extreme of time to the other. With that knowledge, I ran faster—not to hasten the transformation, but to make sure I lived right during the process.

EPILOGUE

Based upon the fact that you are reading this book, you are likely someone who is interested in self-improvement. With that in mind, I encourage you to not lose sight of your lofty goals, because over time, if you take the long view, you can and will succeed, despite any hurdles you may need to overcome to do so.

My grown children accuse me of being the most repetitive man in the world (and I get that!). But, for the last time: Because of journaling and reflective practices, I am able to look back and harvest insights into many of my life decisions and make changes based on what works and what doesn't.

As I have mentioned throughout the book, becoming who you want to be does not usually come easy, and it will not happen overnight. In my case, it required me to take a thirty-five-year detour as a commercial office leasing broker before I became who I wanted to be—a management consultant and coach. Becoming a broker at all was an odd choice for someone who is still challenged by working with numbers.

I mention this because there will always be obstacles for you to overcome in your journey to become who you want to be. If you look at yourself and think that you might be unexceptional in a particular area or that you have certain limitations (like I did), know this: If you make it your thing to control your behavior and do the things you say you're going to do, then you can and will get there!

Knowing that, use the tools presented in this book and enjoy the process of *Becoming Who You Want to Be*.

One of my lifelong commitments has been to share what I've learned with others and help them to have happier and more successful lives. In reading this book, you have helped me make good on that commitment, and I sincerely thank you for it.

THANK YOU!

THE GOOD, THE BAD, AND THE UGLY

October 2010

September 2009

August 2008

| The Good | The Bad |

July 2007

| The Good | The Bad |

June 2006

| The Good | The Bad |

June 2005

| The Good | The Bad |

May 2017

| The Good | (160) | (21.0) |

- Lee Coaching $4000? / Box logic Presentation went well paid 32500/500 each
- Was a Guest Lecturer at NYU - Recived hi Praise / Randy Lippert Visit
- For tree Dispositions / Dinner Landys 1st party
- Denver moves into warehouse / Label/Bar light installed
- Dinner w Mickey - slept there.
- NOLA - Jazz Fest. w Glen & Deb
- House Maintance. / Painted / Pnuemated Sealed - Roof, ect
- Looks Great!
- Cambel Opening / Pre-nice to see Scott & fims / Transplanted Lake Williamberg
- Shingles Shot / Debra / Denver Good meeting / Putthate! Bad Bad hills
- Wiffy love / Laddie Jullie
- Yardwork - Trimmed Hedges / Upstairs office Flowers
- Nice Mother's day - Kids all here / Coaching Jeff with Kelly
- Bruce Blum into Extell / Suzy Reynolds meeting / Bradley / Max
- Colonisky Good Reput? / plants installed $4500 / $7200 / 116 U
- Glen and Deb Visit

January 2011

December 2012

- Finished shade / The Good

| The Bad | | The Ugly |

January 2013

The Good

February 2014

- Lindsane 600d
- Superbowl party
- Sunday am
- Evan co
- Evan
- Evan's 4 yr Anniv
- Box logic - w
- Shipped

| | The Bad | | The Ugly |

April 2016

| The Good | (159) (22) | the bad | The ugly (9) |

March 2015

| The Good | | the Bad | | The Ugly |

- Tracy good work - transaction
- amai

May 2018

| The Good | (33) (157) | The Bad | The Ugly |

- Coached Jon Mantis / Sam Filkins / Cat tu / Sg Att / Leiry Thule In Darren / Brook Max cuts Patterson / Knee - Shoulder / Darren Bladder Cancer
- Lucie - secured an internship / Real Black Day / EVAN BECOMMING W Sales HOME / School Shootings
- w Debra Larsen / Leg Deposit $3147 / Richard / PAINTING GREAT / Leak, Water damage in Basement, Snake lines, couldn't find septic tanks
- Distribution check better than expected w Expansion / Extension / Final check / PH Coaching $5,000 Very Enjoyable Communy Reall Circle / Max Breather Coffee Gull $200 free dinner / PROCEDURE
- massages 46th street heat / massage 57th - Great For Knee
- JAZZ FEST / Lunch John Issacs / Being out of painkiller / Not working out
- Wiffy love / Now Care / Quebec An Steve's 6 on / Next day 1 min Finds take / limping
- Knee Rehab / PORSCHE DELIVERED / All issues Resolved / NO WORKING OUT - Rehab
- Spontanious dinner party fn / $3500 600 V200 / Week 20170 devils Red bridge / $170,000 / 2336 flyde / Watched Lindsay home / Basketball w Evan family
- 13 moved porsche showed Quic party / SNATO REE / ZDEAL ALIVE as consultant / LINDAY HOME all together RETIRED FROM BROKERAGE AFTER 33 (6 not) Years / Being tread for / Uber productive few days. I've posit
- Eti Bin office / MOTHER'S DAY / Kipp w Lindsay / spirit / monk Larsen / funeral SD odd - I hear up daily man who passed / missy new cassitut True Legim
- Happy Vidios shares willie / Fallon Cards Kindness Irish Lucie's Hladant Surf / BILLY DEEBAH Great Catch up / Well stays / Ultimate Lockerbink Mary Ann Griller drove up guy Driveway 25 years later -
- PM Approach / Bradley Visit / Lenise cassistant / Mary Ann Griller (25 later) Day it Forward

ON MY BIRTHDAY + MUSINGS

I'm 51 today and dealing w)

I'm 52 today (yesterday) and feel

I'm 53 Today and Orvolved in — in happiness

I'm 54 today and abound This

I'm 55 today and Basking in

I'm 57 today and basking in the glow of having

I'm 58 today and have such Gratitude for the life

I'm 59 today...

Determine in your mind the outcome of your actions in advance and most often others will come along for the ride as it is often the path of least resistance and takes less energy on their behalf.

1987

By worrying about evaluations made by people who don't know me; I am lending my credence to an incompetent Judge.

1994

1980
I am.
I am doing.
I shall become

I'm today and feeling more

I'm 49 Today and it's a climate of

I'm 48 today. Dealing with June's non

I'm 46 today (last week)

I'm 45 today (

I'm 44 last week and living life that is not consistent

Well I'm 43 today (2 days ago) and am slamming into

I'm 41 Today (last week) struggling with how to act as happy as I am on

I'm 40 today (last week) and

1984

living Retrospect

The greatest enhancement of my life will come with the ability to capture now and Appreciate it as the fond memory it will become.

The Splendor of a moment begins when it is severed from the restricting confine of past and future and let alone to evolve...

1992

I'm 37 ota today. (well last week anyway)

I'm 36 Today (2 weeks ago)

I'm 35 today and

I'm 33 today (6 days ago)

I'm 27 today and once

I'm 26 Today...

I'm today and

I'm 24 day and still experiencing

I'm 23 today after some sadness, handling probleams and ending relationships here I am on my Birthday. I'm supporting myself Paying the bills and appreciate all the Parential support I recieved to get here. I'm in the best shape of my life and am dating several really hot girls. Totally, with no one elses input I've decorated a beautiful apartment and have paid for it myself. I have no real probleams. Drive a brand

The Person you want to be is fantancy now. It slips futher away from reality every time I say I'll Soon change.

LIST OF PAINTINGS

Controlled Chaos
Spray paint on canvas
36 x 36 x 1.5"
2015
Signed on verso

School of Hard Knocks
Acrylic and mixed media on canvas
22 x 28 x 1.5"
2014
Signed on verso

Above the Clouds
Acrylic, oil and spray paint on canvas
48 x 48 x 1.5"
2018
Signed on verso

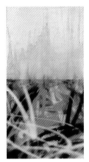

Mystical
Oil and spray paint on canvas
10 x 20 x 1.5"
2018
Signed on verso

Summer Garden
Spray paint on canvas
30 x 30 in
2014
Signed on verso

Untitled 014
Spray paint and plaster on steel
Framed in between plexiglass sheets with brass bolts
15 x 15 x 2.5"
2017
Signed on verso

In Bloom
Acrylic, oil, plaster and spray paint on canvas
36 x 36 x 1.5"
2018
Signed on verso

Untitled 023
Acrylic, oil and spray paint on steel
Framed in between plexiglass sheets with brass bolts
23.5 x 23.5 x 3"
2018
Signed on verso

Premonition
Acrylic, oil, spray paint and resin on canvas
12 x 12 x 1.5"
2018
Signed on verso

Nightmares of the Bottom
Spray paint on canvas
24 x 24 x 1.5"
2018
Signed on verso

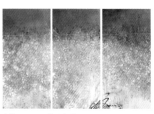

A Midsummer Night's Dream
Acrylic, oil and spray paint on canvas
36 x 54 x 1.5" (Triptych)
2018
Signed on verso

Smooth While Raw
Acrylic, oil and spray paint on canvas
20 x 20 x 1.5"
2018
Signed on verso

Burn After Reading
Acrylic, oil and spray paint on canvas
24 x 30 x 1.5"
2018
Signed on verso

Freefall
Spray paint and acrylic on steel
Framed in between plexiglass sheets with brass bolts
15 x 15 x 2.5"
2017
Signed on verso

Indecision
Oil and spray paint on canvas
36 x 36 x 1.5"
2017
Signed on verso

Dante's Peak
Acrylic, oil, spray paint, resin and mixed media on canvas
12 x 12 x 1.5"
2018
Signed on verso

Blue Dream
Acrylic, oil and spray paint on canvas
12 x 12 x 1.5"
2017
Signed on verso

Awaken My Love
Acrylic and oil on canvas
24 x 30 x 1.5"
2017
Signed on verso

Kaleidoscope Love
Spray paint on canvas
16 x 20 x 1.5"
2018
Signed on verso

Lawless
Spray paint on canvas
24 x 30 x 1.5"
2018
Signed on verso

Untitled 028
Acrylic, oil and spray paint on steel
Framed in between plexiglass sheets with brass bolts
23.5 x 23.5 x 3"
2018
Signed on verso

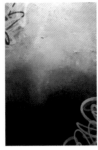

Arrival
Acrylic, oil and spray paint on canvas
30 x 48 x 1.5"
2017
Signed on verso

Supernatural
Acrylic, oil, spray paint and resin on canvas
12 x 12 x 1.5"
2018
Signed on verso

Untitled 024
Acrylic, oil and spray paint on steel
Framed in between plexiglass sheets with brass bolts
23.5 x 23.5 x 3"
2018
Signed on verso

Cowabunga!
Oil stick and spray paint on canvas
36 x 36 x 1.5"
2018
Signed on verso

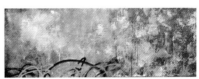

Tragedy & Triumph
Acrylic, oil and spray paint on canvas
60 x 20 x 1.5"
2017
Signed on verso

In My Feelings
Oil stick on canvas
48 x 48 x 1.5"
2018
Signed on verso

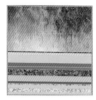

Split Personality
Acrylic and spray paint on canvas
24 x 24 x 1.5"
2018
Signed on verso

Desperado
Acrylic, oil and spray paint on canvas
60 x 48 x 1.5"
2018
Signed on verso

BEZ
Acrylic, oil and spray paint on canvas
40 x 40 x 1.5"
2018
Signed on verso

Fury
Acrylic, oil and spray paint on canvas
20 x 20 x 1.5"
2017
Signed on verso

Breakthrough
Spray paint on canvas
36 x 36 x 1.5"
2018
Signed on verso

Static
Acrylic, oil and spray paint on canvas
48 x 48 x 1.5" (Diptych)
2018
Signed on verso

Untitled 002
Acrylic, oil, plaster and spray paint on steel
Framed in between plexiglass sheets with brass bolts
15 x 15 x 2.5"
2017
Signed on verso

Untitled 006
Acrylic, oil, spray paint and plaster on steel
Framed in between plexiglass sheets with brass bolts
15 x 15 x 2.5"
2017
Signed on verso

Seismic Love
Spray paint and resin on canvas
12 x 12 x 1.5" (Triptych)
2018
Signed on verso

Unruly
Acrylic, oil and spray paint on canvas
36 x 36 x 1.5"
2018
Signed on verso

Ignition
Acrylic, oil and spray paint on canvas
122 x 70 x 1.5"
2018
Signed on verso

Silver Lining
Acrylic, oil and spray paint on canvas
48 x 24 x 1.5"
2017
Signed on verso

Consumed
Oil stick and spray paint on canvas
36 x 36 x 1.5"
2018
Signed on verso

Transpondence
Spray paint on canvas
12 x 12 x 1.5"
2017
Signed on verso

Reflection Eternal
Acrylic, oil and spray paint on canvas
60 x 48 x 1.5"
2018
Signed on verso

SUGGESTED READING

Notes to Myself by Hugh Prather

Notes on Love and Courage by Hugh Prather

The 5 Love Languages by Gary Chapman

Rich Dad Poor Dad by Robert Kiyosaki with Sharon Lechter

Crucial Conversations by Kerry Patterson and Joseph Grenny

How to Be a Gentleman by John Bridges

How to Be a Lady by Candace Simpson-Giles

The Dash by Linda Ellis and Mac Anderson

Who Moved My Cheese? by Spencer Johnson

The Secret by Rhonda Byrne

Man's Search for Meaning by Viktor E. Frankl and William J. Winslade

Invisible Man by Ralph Ellison

Goodbye, Columbus and other works by Philip Roth

Atlas Shrugged by Ayn Rand

The Fountainhead by Ayn Rand

Life of Pi by Yann Martel

Identity by Milan Kundera

Siddhartha by Hermann Hesse

Stumbling on Happiness by Daniel Gilbert

The Three Rooms by Kevin Murphy

ABOUT THE AUTHOR

Gregg Lorberbaum is a management consultant to real estate brokerage firms, an advisor to partnerships and start-ups, and a coach to people in transition.

Gregg is also a general partner in WorkHouse NYC, a co-working company occupying fifteen floors at 21 West 46th Street in Manhattan, with a satellite location at 2 Depot Plaza, adjacent to the Bedford Hills train station. Gregg credits the outstanding success of this venture to his partner, CEO and founder Debra Larsen.

Gregg is the author of *Leasing NYC: The Insider's Guide to Leasing Office Space in Manhattan*. Lois Weiss of the *New York Post* called it "the definitive guide on the subject disguised as a coffee table book." The book won the prestigious Robert Bruss Real Estate Book Silver Medal in 2013.

Gregg lives in Armonk, New York, with his wife, Jill (yes, the girl from second grade), and is the father of three adult children including ELO, the artist.

ABOUT THE ARTIST

Evan Lorberbaum is a visual artist who creates under the moniker ELO, which is short for his movement "Encourage Life Originality." ELO aims to inspire others to reach their full potential in life through embracing their own individuality.

While attending NYU's Gallatin School of Individualized Study (BA '16), his area of concentration was "The Business of Art and Entrepreneurship." During his time at Gallatin he developed a keen, arts-centric interest in branding and marketing. ELO's artistic style and vision is influenced by graffiti, abstract expressionism, and his own relationship with time, personal growth, and pop culture. He is inspired by his modern-day role models: Jay-Z, Shepard Fairey, Marc Ecko, KAWS, Takoshi Murakami, and Pharrell Williams, among others, as he is establishing himself as his own personal brand while blending the lines between art, fashion, and product merchandising.

ELO has been a part of such noteworthy shows as the 2014 New York Regional Semi-Finals of the Bombay Sapphire Artisan Series and a two-month solo exhibition in 2016 at the prestigious Citigroup Center, in conjunction with Boston Properties and the Midtown Arts Common.

In the spring of 2018, the Tambaran2 Gallery presented ELO's New York City solo exhibition, BECOMING. He has also exhibited at the Market Art + Design Hamptons, the Washington Square Outdoor Art Exhibit, and the Armonk Outdoor Art Show. His collaborations/partnerships include brands such as Champs Sports, TOMS, Relevant Customs, Good Wood NYC, Sing For Hope, and FCB Global. His public art project, "What the NYC," aims to

connect New Yorkers through highlighting people, places, and perspectives within New York City. In collaboration with Relevant Customs and Good Wood NYC, ELO created a 1/1 New York City-inspired bespoke sneaker incorporating his original artwork (as well custom patent leather) that pays homage to the spirit of New York City.

From the Artist

My experience as an artist is similar to how we all navigate through our own lives. I am the author and protagonist of my own story. As I add and subtract layers of paint over one another, while scraping through the surface to unmask hidden perspectives, a certain feeling of welcomed unfamiliarity takes over. I am able to embrace this freedom while making the most of the unexpected through this process. The line leads me throughout controlled chaos, as my stream of consciousness guides this narrative, ultimately determining which stroke I will perform and what the canvas will say in this life as I touch others through my work.

Without the support of my family, friends, patrons, and fellow artists, none of my success would be possible. I am becoming the artist I want to be and am excited for what comes next as I continue pursuing this dream.

Tuesday, July 21, 1998
took Jay out ____ to DC by 7:10 - he said all the time. Drove home - Jill thought I look great, morning no new ____ but not really notable - Called in / Enjoyed

Sculpting the land, the stone will not really great! Sauna in lake relaxed. Finished Angelus Ashes.

Wednesday, July 22, 1998
Stayed home again. Late. Enjoyed kids, read relaxed, went to Bathroom the with Jack. Dad relaxed - Don't remember think we grilled out. the land is swimming along. Tony's back ho breaks.

Thursday, July 23, 1998
Got ready for camping - Stayed home - called the office / worked around Enjoyed the kids. Swam in the lake at the Dinner and a movie, sex. But remember

Evan's Campout.

Friday, July 24, 1998
Misty Berger, Jessie Gordon, Louis Rubin set breaks. Mario - Set up Tony's tags pulled thought I did a great job. The stamps were the key to Spa & Shot

Paint Balls. land stiel real saugh. Great time. went to Culdsac Sand. 500 falls chains. Air brushessed. he cooked the trail and was a great help we really meals a good barn also Lindsay was so well behaved.

Sunday, December 26, 1999
up returned at 11:30 Drove home there by 1:00ish. Nice bike home. Basketball w kids - Great fire. Fixed fireplace. Nap. bay w fucus, sleep great. no dinner. Stiel hot + feeling great. ____ Stayed in

Monday, December 27, 1999
Took the day off for Jill / food Shopping Car to Buy w/ - Country Store. Tennis lesson.

☆ New 1957 Cone Vte Bought it! / Jill not on meeting then O.K. - Hay I deserve it. I stayed in at night - OK - Pizza + parties. I had Wine w Bob & Tony. - talked culect ligt3- Spoke to account. Take home ____ ____ ____ Bot on in Basel ofter Taxes, didn't 56ys well. up Punchy about Cave.

August 15, 2000, Tuesday.
Back in the office caught the 6:27 Read E mails, Jurnaland, national phone calls. Turned into a real solid day. Company Meeting Prism was Stellachs #2 National Account! lead from Louis Rubin 10,000 - Robert Rosenfeld 10,000. Mary Jayse Celrod Called. References Marco fei. Both Tom tim & Pete - went really well. Gunderson Deferred $40,000. Ale here Great Materials. Next Ron Burns calls ____

☆ I truly want 1570 for floor - has an offer. Helped Phil was his lead - Invented Driving by Ol house - Heavy Artillery. Spoke to Larker at 6:30 ____ ____ ____ caught 8:30 home by 9:40 Took appoint trip ☆ Cullen't find car keys only 2:00 with

☆ Spoke to Donald Trump. he was ____ him for me.

Then with Bowen as "Moral Support I ugalized Tag ____

I SPOKE IN FRONT ☆ 300 people beautifully powerfully Jill was so proud of me - Great Feel Glad there ☆ Cemetary. Thump Tunes Sittingshiude.
Long Day

Wednesday May 5. 2004.
Sitting Shiva at Junes from 2-8:30. Stephanie, Ally, Jordan, Paul, Mae Come by (Maybe yesterday). Worked from home earlier. Drove in w Jill st 12:00 Quickly to office. So many people came by.

B to B Conference Starts

☆ Katrina ☆
Susan Robb to deliver Back B1312. She work E mail to me - CC ____ ____ New Business Pitch - Using Damn Pike - But I created doubt - Maybe a Co-Broke. Worked. Then Visit Mom. Missed Back to School night. Oh Well - / Evan's teacher love him ☆ ☆

Wednesday, Sept 14 2005
Woak up at 6:10

Bat exi, Miss ☆ Volunteer ☆

last minute thing with Jeff Tanner - Haw Have to airpart - ____ then left behind (bad decision) Phil

Great time w Jeff Tanneddew

☆ Start of my own Brokerage in Koman DC LA

Wednesday, Oct 4, 2006.
So Bummed, but handling it better. Discussed situation w Peter T. Great to have a guy like him around. Met w David Michaeli of Coldwel banker. Wore a Suit feeling pretty good That situation is not for me. What a great account for 6L RE 25-30,000 sq. ft. relocation - Felt Great - No jordan. Met w Daniel.

Set up 6L RE at luck and web-site for Greg's Glreal.com. - Solid defensive step! - back feeling better. home in early.

Thursday, Oct 5, 2006
Well, a better day in some ways - worse in others. Audi Service $850 take - Breakfast w Larry Laseure - He like the offers Jordan, Ally, are not there for me. I guess I should not be surprised. Worked on E mails ____ about not holding up my commissions. Time w Daniel and Wanda - then ____ Stopt at Imperial House - Everything will break out OK But must have Discipline!

Lexington - 25,000
McKeel - 11,000
Komar - 3200 1/2 - 2yrs
Mayer - Dead Deal

Saturday, November 19, 2011
Solid day. Weight workout, massage Rosalinda. Cleaned up Stinkfire team office. - Organized Garage tailor - Found out **LINDSAY ACCEPTED to TULANE !!** huda- I cried - ____ home to hug her - Relaxed Read News Papers - Dinner ____ Sarrani Birthday: / Paid $180

Sunday, November 20, 2011
Relaxing day / hour eliptical. Breakfast w Jill. Got gas. filled drive vette. - Manicure, massage ____ Jill home. Watched Football, napped + empower. Family Dinner at MIA.

Monday, November 21, 2011
Up, ____ ____ Solid weight workout then more ____. to city. Tracy up to the w ille hole in her pants - trendy Bar then met w Austin - Meeting Prep

Tuesday, October 30, 2012
☆ SANDY AFTERMATH ☆ Up early. After Cold night w No Power 6:30 am - out to Generator. Panell down - Bummer. Pushed Button.

IT STARTED !!! **Yeahh !!!** ____ Grattuly **I DON'T FEEL STUPID !** (anymore) rest of Day - relaxed approved Book Jacket / Basically relaxed and basked in the Glow of Power. Watched a movie w Evan- ate Lucie had friend Danny Spee Race around Barbon - beautiful like after meeting - GRATITUDE - and nothing to ____ about - A True day of ☆

Wednesday - Oct 31, 2012
An off day - 2/3 of math of Sandy Shit - City shut down. no work to be done ☆

L A
very confident - Company at ____ - This next yr 10+ target 13MM. 30+ re turn - 100,000 MM Not enough humm. - I have ____ Great breakfast - hey 6 yrs. later were still "Be violent Time will tell - then BoG Drove us to Susan Roth - lunch in her building - Great to see her. - then - back - had a massage - Mexican Dinner at really cozy place - Walked around Balboa Island after meeting - beautiful life. home - tired of ter. BASKETBALL game. Loyola - exciting game 7 Cenka - kids play D+ Ball next year - Nice evening

Saturday, February 23 2013
up to last 1/2 day - Great Trip

but I'm excited to get home. Great Walk w Merelle and Bob on the beach - then ate breakfast on the beach. Called Jill, miss her - then a little rushed - Picked up Car - Convertable - Top down - finally a nice day - Met Wendy and Jeff at Moon - Struck - beautiful ocean view - really enjoyable Then off to - the Air Port - DID NOT GET LOST ONCE - Eailier read ☆ On Tice - The Pacific Instinct humm - my calling? - LONG Nice Flight home. empty seat next to me - Picked up Taxi to Garage - Picked up Stuff at Sharon's - Drove from home feelt to pay feel that like!

Sunday February 24, 2013
Great day of Enjoying being home - to me →